Quick & Easy

DIM SUM
APPETIZERS
AND
LIGHT MEALS

Co-Published by Japan Publications Co., Ltd and Joie, Inc.

Distributors:
United States:
Kodansha America, Inc., through Oxford University Press
198 Madison Avenue, New York, NY 10016
Canada:
Fitzhenry & Whiteside Ltd.
195 Allstate Parkway, Markham, Ontario L3R 4T8
Australia and New Zealand:
Bookwise International Pty Ltd.
174 Cormack Road, Wingfield, SA 5013 Australia
Asia and other countries:
Japan Publications Trading Co., Ltd., 1-2-1 Sarugaku-cho, Chiyoda-ku, Tokyo, 101-0064 Japan

First Edition July 2007
Original Copyright © 2007 by Judy Lew
World rights reserved by JOIE, INC. 1-8-3, Hirakawa-cho, Chiyoda-ku, Tokyo 102-0093 Japan
Printed in Japan

ISBN:978-4-88996-226-0

ACKNOWLEDGMENTS

With the greatest respect and most sincere admiration for my publisher, Mr. Shiro Shimura, I thank you for your immeasurable patience and understanding. Your trust and belief in my work has provided me with great enthusiasm to proceed with commitment and dedication. I am very proud to be associated with JOIE, Inc.

To my editor, Mr. Akira Naito, my deepest gratitude and a very special thank you for your enduring patience and kind understanding of my schedule. I am very lucky to have such a wonderful editor, for you deserve only "star" status and you are the best.

And to Yukiko-san, thank you for always trying to keep me on track. Thank you for some of my most treasured accomplishments, you are the driving force always. To you, my most sincere and fond thank you.

A special thank you to Ms. Sumiko Kobayashi and the JOIE editorial staff for all the hard work and organization involved in the production of this book.

To Mr. Tomio Moriguchi, president of Uwajimaya Inc., my warmest thoughts are to my beginning. Thank you for all of the opportunities and your commitment to my work.

My appreciation of Mr. George Nakauye's talents as my pthotographer, transcends any thank you. Your commitment of time and energy makes you a very special friend always.

I would like to express my appreciation for all of the assistance from Ms. Nam Lew, for through her, some of the best recipes evolved. Her expertise in Chinese cooking has been a very valuable resource.

To Willkie, Kimberley and Pamela, my love to you always.

And finally to my parents, thank you for all of the countless times I enjoyed dim sum with you, the family and friends. To understand the love shared during those times is to understand the true meaning of dim sum. You will always continue to touch my heart.

ENJOY!

INTRODUCTION

Since the 10th. century A.D. Sung dynasy, the Chinese have enjoyed eating tasty, delicate, little dumplings called Dim Sum. Iinitially there were only a few choices to choose from, found mainly in tea houses which people frequented for an afternoon chat or business. As demand and popularity spread so did the menus and selections.

Southern China favored small delicate steamed buns, dumplings and pastries, such as cha siu bao (steamed pork buns). Eastern provinces (Nanking and Shanghai) were known for their duck, seafood, and fish dishes. People from this region usually prefer slow cooked foods. Fukien is known for its soups and bean-curd and pancakes wrapped around tasty morsals of food.

In Northern China where it is difficult to grow rice wheat is substituted and used as a base in noodles, buns, pancakes, breads and cakes. Vinegar is often used as a seasoning, giving us sweet and sour dishes as well as the world famous Peking Duck. The food from the north is lighter and milder compared to the heavier and spicier foods of the western provinces such as Szechuan and Hunan. These provinces use a lot of red and green peppers with the belief that they stimulate the palate and enhance the subtle range of flavours found in food.

Due to the scarcity of ovens and fuel in China dim sum are made by shaping dough into tiny bite sized pieces instead of loaves, so that they will cook quickly. They are usually steamed, deep fried or pan fried and served accompanied with tea.

The Cantonese brought dim sum to the American China towns in the 1800's and today more and more restaurants are catering to dim sum diners and are becoming more and more popular, with typical menu sometimes offering as many as 50 different choices.

All over the world one can witness scenes of dim sum feasting. From Hong Kong to London to San Francisco to New York, early mornings through late nights and especially weekends, although the most popular times are between 11 a.m. and 3 p.m. During these hectic hours the number and variety of customers often match the many choices that are available!

Traditionaly waiters will push trolley carts full of delicacies and customers will stop the waiters and order straight from the carts, each plate costs the same, so the waiter just counts the number of dishes on your table and hands you the bill/check.

Dim Sum are an important part of Chinese life, not only on a daily basis but also at various festivals throughout the year. The purpose of this book is to introduce you, step by step to the processes and techniques involved in making Dim Sum, hopefully giving you a more personal and rewarding experience, while learning more about Chinese culture.

Judy Lew

DEDICATION

TO MY MOTHER, FATHER AND THE LOVED
ONES I HOLD DEAREST TO MY HEART

CONTENTS

CONTENTS

METRIC TABLES

★ 1 cup is equivalent to 240 ml in our recipes: (American cup measurement)

    1 American cup = 240 ml = 8 American fl oz

    1 British cup = 200 ml = 7 British fl oz

    1 Japanese cup = 200 ml

1 tablespoon = 15 ml   1 teaspoon = 5 ml

T = tablespoon	t = teaspoon	C = Cup
fl = fluid	oz = ounce	lb = pound
ml = milliliter	g = gram	cm = centimeter
F = Fahrenheit	C = Celsius	

TABLES CONVERTING FROM U.S. CUSTOMARY SYSTEM TO METRICS

Liquid Measures

U.S. Customary system	oz	g	ml
$^1/_{16}$ cup = 1 T	$^1/_2$ oz	14 g	15 ml
$^1/_4$ cup = 4 T	2 oz	60 g	59 ml
$^1/_2$ cup = 8 T	4 oz	115 g	118 ml
1 cup = 16 T	8 oz	225 g	236 ml
$1^3/_4$ cups	14 oz	400 g	414 ml
2 cups = 1 pint	16 oz	450 g	473 ml
3 cups	24 oz	685 g	710 ml
4 cups	32 oz	900 g	946 ml

Liquid Measures

Japanese system	oz	ml
$^1/_8$ cup	$^7/_8$ oz	25 ml
$^1/_4$ cup	$1^3/_4$ oz	50 ml
$^1/_2$ cup	$3^1/_2$ oz	100 ml
1 cup	7 oz	200 ml
$1^1/_2$ cups	$10^1/_2$ oz	300 ml
2 cups	14 oz	400 ml
3 cups	21 oz	600 ml
4 cups	28 oz	800 ml

Weights

ounces to grams *
$^1/_4$ oz = 7 g
$^1/_2$ oz = 14 g
1 oz = 30 g
2 oz = 60 g
4 oz = 115 g
6 oz = 170 g
8 oz = 225 g
16 oz = 450 g

* Equivalent

Linear Measures

inches to centimeters
$^1/_2$ in = 1.27 cm
1 in = 2.54 cm
2 in = 5.08 cm
4 in = 10.16 cm
5 in = 12.7 cm
10 in = 25.4 cm
15 in = 38.1 cm
20 in = 50.8 cm

Temperatures

Fahrenheit (F) to Celsius (C)		
freezer storage	−10°F =	−23.3°C
	0°F =	−17.7°C
water freezes	32°F =	0 °C
	68°F =	20 °C
	100°F =	37.7°C
water boils	212°F =	100 °C
	300°F =	148.8°C
	400°F =	204.4°C

Deep-Frying Oil Temperatures

300°F − 330°F (150°C − 165°C) = low
340°F − 350°F (170°C − 175°C) = moderate
350°F − 360°F (175°C − 180°C) = high

Conversion Factor

$$C = F - 32 \times {}^5/_9$$

$$F = \frac{C \times 9}{5} + 32$$

BASIC HINTS

1. Read each recipe carefully to understand each step, as dim sum preparation requires extensive hand work. If the formation of a dumpling seems difficult at first, try to shape it in an easier style, it will taste just as delicious.

2. Have all ingredients cut and organized before the cooking process. This will make cooking much easier and faster so foods will not be over cooked once you begin.

3. Use the bamboo steamer to steam bread type dim sum. The ventilation of the bamboo keeps condensation inside the steamer to a minimum and breads do not get wet.

4. The selection of hot sauces is vast. Choose the one most pleasing to yourself to accompany the dim sum choices. Chinese hot mustard is always a popular choice. Hot mustard comes in a powder. Measure 1 tablespoon of powder and add 2 tablespoons of water and stir until a smooth paste is formed. Often soy sauce is added and used as a dip.

5. All the recipes in this book can be made by using a good quality Japanese all purpose soy sauce. Japanese soy sauce can be purchased in all grocery stores in the Asian foods section.

6. The use of the proper utensils makes the task of Dim Sum preparation much easier. A good quality cleaver is most important as the cutting and chopping must be done before the cooking process begins. Also it is required for the formation of certain types of dumplings.

7. Dim Sum should be enjoyed with as many people as possible. This allows for more selections of appetizers to be sampled.

8. Dim Sum dining also includes many noodle dishes. Refer to the cookbooks, such as "Enjoy Chinese Cuisine" and "Enjoy the Flavors of Chinese Cooking by Judy Lew" for more noodle recipes.

BASIC BUN DOUGH

⟨INGREDIENTS: Makes 16 buns⟩

2 T	dry yeast
1/4 C	warm water (110°F, 43°C)
1/2 C	warm milk
1 T	sugar
1/4 C	melted butter
1/4 C	sugar
1/2 t	salt
2	large eggs (room temp.)
3 ~ 3 1/2 C	all purpose flour

This dough is tender and delicious for all baked bread recipes such as rolls or filled breads.

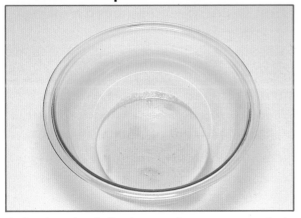

1. In a large bowl, dissolve yeast in warm water and stir in sugar. Let stand 5 minutes.

2. Combine warm milk, melted butter, sugar, salt and eggs. Add to yeast mixture. Beat together.

3. Add 3C of flour and gradually mix.

4. Turn dough onto a floured surface and knead until smooth, working in the remaining 1/2C flour (approx. 10 minutes).

5. Place dough in a greased bowl, cover and let rise until doubled in size.

6. Dough has doubled in volume.

7. Punch down dough.

8. Knead 2 minutes and allow to rest 2 minutes before shaping into desired rolls.

PORK AND CHINESE SAUSAGE BUNS

For a light meal, good as an alternative for sandwiches.

⟨**INGREDIENTS: Makes 16 buns**⟩

Filling

1 T	oil
1 C	ground pork
2	Chinese sausages, chopped finely
½ C	chopped onions
2 T	soy sauce
1 T	hoisin sauce
1 T	catsup
1 T	rice wine
1 t	sugar
1 T	sesame seed oil
1	chopped green onion

1 T	cornstarch dissolved in ¼ C water
1	quantity Basic Bun Dough (p 10)
16	2″ × 2″ (5 × 5 cm) squares waxed paper
2 T	butter (to brush over buns)

1. Prepare vegetables and sausages.

2. Heat wok, add oil and stir-fry pork until done. Add sausage and all other ingredients, cook for ¹/₂ minute.

3. Add cornstarch mixture and bring to a full boil. Toss in green onions. Set aside and allow to cool.

4. Divide dough into 16 equal pieces and fill each with approx. 2 T filling. Place on a piece of waxed paper and arrange on a baking sheet.

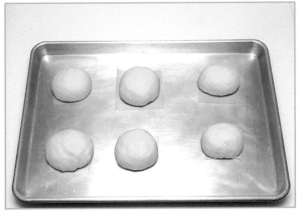

5. Allow to rise until doubled in size. Bake in 375°F (190°C) oven until golden brown (approx. 15 minutes).

6. Remove from oven and brush with butter to keep surface soft.

SAUSAGE ROLLS

Other types of sausage can be used.

⟨**INGREDIENTS: Makes 4 rolls**⟩

4	Chinese sausages
$^{1}/_{2}$	quantity Basic Bun Dough (p 10)
2 T	butter
4	(2″ × 6″) (5 × 15 cm) waxed paper

1. Steam sausages for 15 minutes in a steamer. Allow to cool.

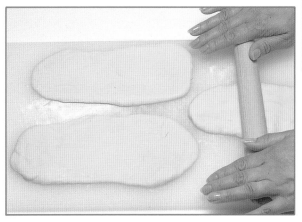

2. Divide dough into 4 equal pieces. Roll each out into an 8″ × 3″ (20 × 8 cm) rectangle.

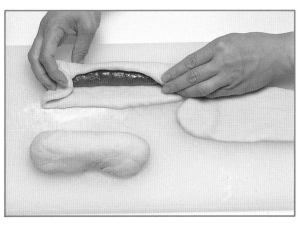

3. Place 1 Chinese sausage on dough and wrap tucking under edges of dough.

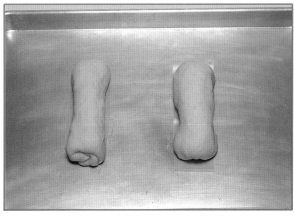

4. Place roll on a piece of waxed paper and arrange on a baking sheet. Allow to double in size.

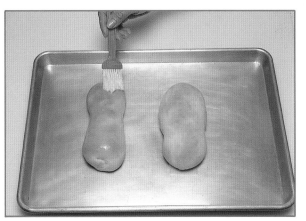

5. Bake at 350°F (175°C) for 15 minutes or until golden brown. Remove from oven and brush with butter. Slice into 1″ (2.5 cm) pieces before serving.

CURRY PORK BUNS

Curry chicken is a good variation.

⟨INGREDIENTS: Makes 16 buns⟩

Filling

1 T	oil
1 C	ground pork
2	Chinese sausages, finely chopped
½ C	chopped onions
1 T	curry powder
2 T	soy sauce
1 T	catsup
1 T	rice wine
1 t	sugar
1 T	sesame seed oil

1 T	cornstarch dissolved in ¼C water.
1	quantity Basic Bun Dough (p 10)
16	2″ × 2″ (5 × 5 cm) squares waxed paper
2 T	butter (to brush over buns)

1. Prepare vegetables and sausages.

2. Heat wok, add oil and stir-fry pork until done, remove excess oil. Add sausage and all other ingredients, cook for ½ minute.

3. Add cornstarch mixture and bring to a full boil. Set aside to cool.

4. Divide dough into 16 equal pieces and fill each with approx. 2 T filling. Place on a piece of waxed paper.

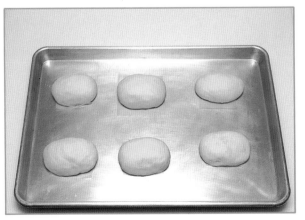

5. Allow to rise until doubled in size. Bake in 375°F (190°C) oven until golden brown (approx. 15 minutes).

6. Remove from oven and brush with butter to keep surface soft.

SWEET BEAN PASTE BUNS 甜豆沙包

A delicious sweet bread to serve with coffee or tea.

〈INGREDIENTS: Makes 16 buns〉

1   quantity Basic Bun Dough (p10)
1   18 oz can sweet bean paste
16   2″ × 2″ (5 × 5 cm) squares waxed paper
2 T butter

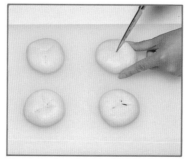

1. Prepare 1 recipe of basic bun dough and divide into 16 equal pieces. Divide sweet bean paste into 16 equal portions.

2. Flatten each piece of dough into a 4″ (10 cm) round: allow to rest for 2 minutes while shaping the other pieces of dough. Place bean paste in center of dough and close off by gathering and pleating the edges together. Place on waxed paper.

3. Press the top of bun to flatten. Cut 3 slits on top of bun. Bake at 350°F (175°C) for 15 minutes or until golden brown. Remove from oven and brush with butter.

MINI BARBECUED PORK SANDWICHES 小叉燒三文治

Favorite for buffet party.

〈INGREDIENTS: Makes 15 pieces〉

1/2	quantity Basic Bun Dough (p10)
1/2 lb (225 g)	cooked barbecued pork, sliced
4	lettuce leaves
1/2 C	sliced red pepper
1/2 C	sliced cucumber
2	green onions, sliced

Dips
Plum sauce
Hoisin sauce

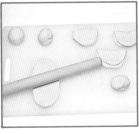

1. Divide dough into 2″ (5 cm) balls and roll out into an oval. Fold oval over and place on a baking sheet.

2. Bake at 350°F (175°C) for 15 minutes.

3. Remove from oven and brush tops with butter.

4. To serve: Open rolls and brush with choice of sauce. Place barbecued pork slices, cucumber, peppers and green onions inside. Eat as a sandwich.

19

STEAMED BARBECUED PORK BUNS

Other fillings can be used.

〈INGREDIENTS: Makes 16 buns〉

Filling

¹/₂ T	oil
¹/₄ C	diced onions
¹/₂	large forest mushroom (soaked, rinsed and diced)
1 T	hoisin sauce
1 T	catsup
³/₄ T	sugar
¹/₂ T	oyster sauce
¹/₈ t	garlic powder
¹/₄ t	salt
¹/₄ C	water
¹/₂ T	cornstarch dissolved in 1T water
³/₄ C	diced cooked barbecued pork

Dough

¹/₂ C	warm water
1 T	sugar
2 T	dry yeast
³/₄ C	warm milk
¹/₂ C	sugar
3～3¹/₂ C	all purpose flour
¹/₂ t	salt
16	pieces waxed paper (3 × 3″, 8 × 8cm each)

NOTE
Filling may be made ahead. Freeze unused portion.

How To Make Filling

1. Add oil to wok, cook onions and mushrooms on high heat for ¹/₂ minute.

2. Add all other ingredients, except cornstarch and barbecued pork, Allow to cook ¹/₂ minute.

3. Thicken with cornstarch mixture to form a thick sauce. Mix in diced pork: cool.

How To Make Bun Dough

1. In a large bowl, dissolve 1T sugar and yeast in warm water. Allow mixture to sit 5 minutes.

2. Combine warm milk with ½C sugar, stir to dissolve sugar. Add to yeast mixture.

3. Combine 3C of flour with salt. Stir into liquid yeast mixture.

4. Stir until a firm dough is formed. Turn out on floured surface and knead until smooth, adding extra flour if necessary (about 10 minutes).

5. Place in a greased bowl, turn dough over and cover with a towel. Allow to rise until doubled in bulk.

6. Dough is doubled in volume.

7. Punch down dough, knead 2 minutes and allow to rest 2 minutes. Cut into 16 equal pieces.

8. Roll each piece into a ball, then roll into a 4″ (10cm) circle, dusting with flour if necessary. Allow dough to rest 2 minutes. Roll out other pieces while waiting. Place 1T filling in center.

9. Pull dough over filling and close top by pleating, pinching and twisting edges together.

10. Place on a piece of waxed paper, pleated edge down. Space 2″ (5cm) apart on a steaming plate. Allow to rise 45 minutes in a warm oven (95°F, 35°C).

11. Steam in wok for 15 minutes at full steam. Remove cover carefully so water will not drop on top of buns.

21

PORK AND CHICKEN ROLLS

Delicious with a sweet and sour sauce.

⟨INGREDIENTS: Makes 3 rolls⟩

Pastry

1¹/₂ C	all purpose flour	
1 T	sugar	
¹/₈ t	salt	
¹/₂ C	cold butter	
1	egg yolk	
2 T	cold water	

Filling

¹/₂ lb (225 g)	ground pork or chicken or combination
2 T	chopped onions
1 T	rice wine

1 T	soy sauce
	Pinch of salt
¹/₂ t	sugar
2 t	cornstarch
	Green and red peppers (optional)

GLAZE

1	egg yolk
1 t	soy sauce

1. Combine filling ingredients, set aside.

2. Combine flour, sugar and salt in a bowl. Cut in butter to resemble coarse oatmeal. Leave mixture fairly coarse.

3. Combine egg yolk and cold water. Beat together just until combined.

4. Add egg mixture to flour mixture and stir with a fork to moisten.

5. Flour mixture should just come together. Add a little more water if mixture is too dry.

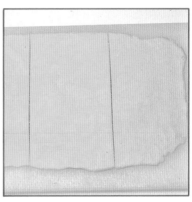

6. Roll out crust 8″ × 14″ (20 × 35 cm) and cut into thirds.

7. Place ⅓ of filling ingredients in center of crust. Roll up crust, sealing sides and bottom.

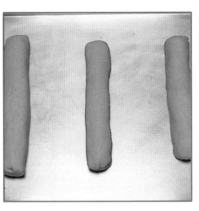

8. Place on a baking sheet and bake at 375°F (190°C) for 25 minutes. Brush tops with egg yolk mixed with 1t soy sauce.

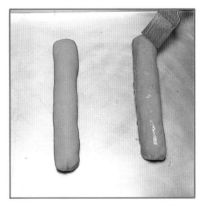

9. Remove and allow to cool. Slice into 1″ (2.5 cm) pieces before serving.

CURRY TRIANGLES

A very delicate and tender pastry.

⟨INGREDIENTS: Makes 22⟩

Filling

	¹/₂ lb (225g)	boneless chicken breast, minced
Ⓐ {	1 T	sesame seed oil
	1 T	soy sauce
	1 T	rice wine
	1 T	cornstarch
	1 t	sugar
	1 t	finely minced peeled fresh ginger root
	1	garlic clove, minced

1 T oil
¹/₂ C minced onions
2 t curry powder
2 T oyster sauce
¹/₂ t sugar
1 T rice wine
1 T cornstarch dissolved in ¹/₃ C chicken stock

Pastry

1¹/₂ C all purpose flour
1 T sugar
¹/₈ t salt
¹/₂ C cold butter
1 egg yolk
2 T cold water

Glaze

1 egg yolk
1 t soy sauce

1. Toss chicken with ingredients Ⓐ. Let stand 2 hours. Heat wok over high heat, add oil. Stir-fry chicken and onions until chicken is opaque.

2. Add remaining ingredients, bring to a boil and thicken with dissolved cornstarch mixture. (Can be prepared ahead).

3. Combine flour, sugar and salt in a bowl. Cut in butter to resemble coarse oatmeal. Leave mixture fairly coarse.

4. Combine egg yolk and cold water. Beat together just until combined.

5. Add egg mixture to flour mixture and stir with a fork to moisten. Flour mixture should just come together. Add a little more water if mixture is too dry.

6. Cover and chill mixture for 15 minutes. Turn dough out onto a lightly floured surface. Gently knead just to smooth out.

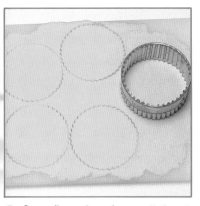

7. On a floured surface, roll dough into a ¼″ (1 cm) thick sheet and cut out 4″ (10 cm) rounds. Use flour to keep fingers from sticking during handling of dough. Place 2T filling in center of round.

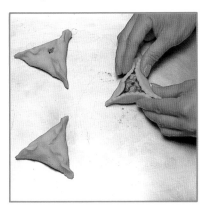

8. Bring up edges to form a triangle. Can also be made into a crescent by folding round in half and crimp edges to seal. Place on a baking sheet, brush with glaze. Bake at 375°F (190°C) until golden brown (25 ~ 30 minutes).

MEATS

Stir-fry the meat first in the wok with a small amount of oil. Remove meat, then cook vegetables adding the meat back in to retain tenderness without over cooking the meat. This technique is often used when the meat and vegetables require different cooking times.

STUFFED BELL PEPPERS WITH BLACK BEAN SAUCE 釀辣椒豆豉糊

Delicious when served with rice.

⟨INGREDIENTS: 4~6 servings⟩

1/2 lb (225g)	bell peppers (green, red, and yellow)	1/2	egg white
		2 T	oil for pan-frying stuffed peppers
Shrimp Filling		**Sauce**	
1/2 lb (225g)	peeled, cleaned shrimp, chopped (other seafoods can be used)	1 T	oil
		2 T	salted black beans, rinsed and drained
2 T	chopped bamboo shoots	2 t	grated fresh ginger root
1 T	chopped fresh water chestnuts	2 t	minced fresh garlic
		1/2 t	sugar
1 T	rice wine	1 T	wine
1 t	sesame seed oil	2 T	soy sauce
1/2 t	salt	1 T	cornstarch
1 T	cornstarch	1 C	rich chicken stock

NOTE

Using red, yellow, and green bell peppers create a very nice color combination in the presentation of the recipe.

1. Cut bell peppers into quarters, lengthwise. Remove seeds and cut into 2″ (5 cm) pieces. Combine filling ingredients and spoon into pepper pieces. Keep filling approx. 1/2″ (1.5 cm) thick, gently forcing into grooves of peppers.

2. Heat a large skillet and add 2T oil. Slowly pan-fry stuffed pepper pieces, meat side only on medium high heat. Cover skillet for faster cooking. Reduce temperature if meat browns too soon (approx. 4 minutes). Use a non-stick skillet for this step. Transfer to small individual plates (3~4 pieces per plate).

3. In a small sturdy bowl, mash black beans, ginger, garlic, and sugar together to form a smooth paste. Using the same skillet, add 1T oil. Fry the black bean mixture on medium high heat until fragrant (approx. 1/2 minute). Combine remaining ingredients and stir until cornstarch is dissolved. Add to black bean mixture and bring to a full boil stirring constantly (Add 1~2t of chili paste with black beans for a spicy hot sauce). Spoon sauce over cooked stuffed peppers before serving.

STUFFED EGGPLANTS WITH BLACK BEAN SAUCE 釀茄豆豉糊

A dim sum favorite.

⟨INGREDIENTS: 4~6 servings⟩

1/2 lb (225g)	Japanese eggplants (cut into 10 pieces)
Shrimp Filling	
1/2 lb (225g)	peeled, cleaned shrimp, chopped (other seafoods can be used)
2 T	chopped bamboo shoots
1 T	chopped fresh water chestnuts
1 T	rice wine
1 t	sesame seed oil
1/2 t	salt
1 T	cornstarch

1/2	egg white
2 T	oil for pan-frying stuffed eggplants
Sauce	
1 T	oil
2 T	salted black beans, rinsed and drained
2 t	grated fresh ginger root
2 t	minced fresh garlic
1/2 t	sugar
1 T	*mirin* (sweet rice wine)
2 T	soy sauce
1 T	cornstarch
1 C	rich chicken stock

1. Slice eggplants diagonally into 1″ (2.5 cm) thick slices. Cut each slice in the center leaving 1/2″ (1.5 cm) held together.

2. Combine filling ingredients and gently force into eggplant, approx. 1/2″ (1.5 cm) thick.

3. Heat a large skillet and add 2T oil. Pan-fry eggplant slowly, covered, for 4 to 5 minutes. Turn eggplant as needed. (Use a non-stick skillet for this step.) Transfer to small individual plates (2~3 pieces per plate).

4. In a small sturdy bowl, mash black beans, ginger, garlic, and sugar together to form a smooth paste. Using the same skillet, add 1T oil. Fry the black bean mixture on medium high heat until fragrant (approx. 1/2 minute). Combine remaining ingredients and stir until cornstarch is dissolved. Add to black bean mixture and bring to a full boil stirring constantly (Add 1~2t of chili paste with black beans for a spicy hot sauce). Spoon sauce over cooked stuffed eggplants before serving.

BRAISED SPARERIBS WITH BLACK BEAN SAUCE 豆豉炒排骨

Serve with a stir-fried vegetable dish for a complete menu.

⟨INGREDIENTS: 4～6 servings⟩

1 T	oil
1 lb (450g)	pork spareribs cut into 1¹/₂″ (4 cm) pieces

Sauce

2 T	salted black beans
2 t	fresh minced garlic
2 t	fresh minced ginger root
1 t	sugar
1 t	soy sauce

1 t	rice wine
1 C	water
1 T	cornstarch dissolved in ¹/₄C water for thickening

Chopped green onions for garnish

1. Heat wok and add 1T oil. Stir-fry spareribs for 3 minutes and drain off excess oil.

2. Add sauce ingredients and fry for ¹/₂ minute. Add water, cover, and cook for twenty minutes.

3. Thicken with cornstarch mixture to make a medium thick sauce. Garnish with green onions.

STEAMED SPARERIBS OVER RICE 蒸排骨飯

A very easy complete meal.

〈INGREDIENTS: 4 servings〉
5 C cooked white rice
1 quantity Braised Spareribs with Black Bean Sauce (p 28)

1. Divide rice into 4 equal portions and place in heat proof bowls. Top with spareribs and place in a steamer.

2. Steam for 10 to 15 minutes or until all ingredients are heated through. Garnish with green onions or parsley.

NOTE
Mix in 1T chili paste to make spareribs spicy.

Steamed or deep-fried, very good with hot mustard sauce.

⟨INGREDIENTS: Makes 30⟩

30	Siu Mai wrappers	2	large forest mushrooms chopped (soaked and rinsed)
Filling			
1 lb (450g)	coarse ground pork	1½ t	salt
1	Chinese sausage, chopped	½ t	sugar
2 T	chopped bamboo shoots	1 t	wine
2 T	chopped water chestnuts	1 t	sesame seed oil
¼ C	chopped onion	1 t	soy sauce
		2 T	cornstarch

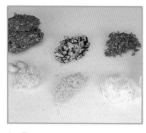

1. Prepare vegetables and sausage.

2. Combine all filling ingredients.

3. Place 1T filling in center of wrapper. Gather edge of wrapper around filling. Flatten the bottom, squeeze the center and smooth off top with wet fingers.

4. Place on steaming plate ½″ (1.5cm) apart. Steam for 20 minutes.

STEAMED SWEET RICE SIU MAI 燒賣糯米飯

Serve with any meat dish.

⟨INGREDIENTS: Makes 25⟩

1   quantity Treasured Sweet Rice (p 72)
25 Siu Mai wrappers
Chopped parsley, or green onions for garnish

1. Place 1T rice in center of wrapper.

2. Close wrapper around rice pressing the rice into center. Smooth off top.

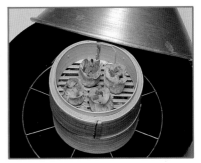

3. Place in a steamer ½″ (1.5 cm) apart and steam for 5 to 6 minutes on high heat. Garnish with parsley or green onions.

FOUR COLOR SIU MAI 四色燒賣

Other ingredients in contrasting color may be added.

⟨INGREDIENTS: Makes 25⟩

Filling

¹/₂ lb (225g)	ground pork
2 T	chopped bamboo shoots
2 T	chopped water chestnuts
1 T	soy sauce
¹/₂ t	sugar
1 t	sesame seed oil
2 T	cornstarch
1 T	rice wine

Topping

¹/₄ C	chopped cooked Chinese black mushrooms
¹/₄ C	chopped ham
¹/₄ C	chopped green pepper
¹/₄ C	chopped yellow pepper or cooked egg yolk
25	Sui Mai wrappers

Other suggested toppings: mushrooms, carrots, egg, ham, green pepper, yellow pepper, green beans, red pepper.

1. Prepare vegetables and ham.

2. Combine filling ingredients and allow to marinate for 1 hour in refrigerator.

3. Place 1T level filling on each siu mai wrapper. Close wrapper by pinching in half, then into quarters, forming 4 small cups on top.

4. Fill cups with small amounts of selected topping ingredients. Place in a steamer, each ¹/₂″ (1.5cm) apart and cook for 6 to 8 minutes on high heat.

CHICKEN SIU MAI　鷄肉燒賣

A good variation to use with other meats or seafood.

⟨INGREDIENTS: Makes 25⟩

¹/₂ lb (225g)	boneless chicken breast, chopped
¹/₄ C	chopped bamboo shoots
¹/₄ C	chopped Chinese black mushrooms
2 T	chopped water chestnuts
1 T	rice wine
2 T	cornstarch
¹/₂	egg white

1 T	soy sauce
1 T	sesame seed oil
1 t	sugar
¹/₂ t	salt
¹/₄ t	white pepper
25	Siu Mai wrappers

NOTE
Filling can be made a day ahead and refrigerated.

1. Prepare vegetables.

2. Combine thoroughly all filling ingredients making sure all ingredients are dispersed well (Allow mixture to set in refrigerator for 1 hour for better flavor).

3. Spread 2T filling ingredients on a wrapper and pleat the sides to surround meat. Wet fingers to smooth off top of siu mai.

4. Place in a steamer, each ¹/₂″ (1.5 cm) apart and steam for 10 minutes on high heat.

PORK AND CHINESE SAUSAGE DUMPLINGS 豬肉臘腸餃

Any meats or vegetable filling can be used.

⟨ **INGREDIENTS: Makes 25** ⟩

1	quantity of wheat starch dough, (p 76)	½ C chopped shrimp
Filling		2 T soy sauce
1 T	oil	2 T rice wine
½ lb (225g)	ground pork	½ t sugar
1	Chinese sausage, finely diced	1 green onion, chopped
¼ C	chopped preserved turnips	
¼ C	chopped water chestnuts	

1. Heat wok on high heat, add oil and stir-fry pork until done. Add Chinese sausage and remaining ingredients. Combine thoroughly and mix in green onions.

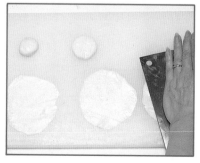

2. Prepare 1 recipe of wheat starch dough. Roll dough into a long roll and cut into walnut size pieces. Roll each piece in hand until a smooth ball forms. Generously oil cutting board and cleaver. Press out dough to form a 3″ (8cm) circle.

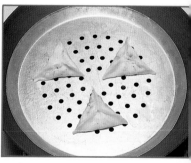

3. Place 1T of filling in the center of circle and close circle forming a triangle. Place on an oiled steamer and steam for 10 minutes on medium high heat.

34

SHRIMP AND PORK DUMPLINGS 蝦豬肉餃

⟨INGREDIENTS: Makes 20⟩

Filling

1/3 lb (150g)	shrimp, shelled, deveined and chopped
1/3 lb (150g)	ground pork
2	black mushrooms, soaked, rinsed and chopped
1/4 C	chopped bamboo shoots
1/4 C	green peas, or chopped green onions
1 T	sesame seed oil
1/2 t	sugar
1 t	salt
1/2 t	white pepper
1	egg white
2 T	cornstarch

Dough

1 C	wheat starch
1/2 C	tapioca starch
1/2 t	salt
1 C	boiling water
2 t	oil

Use other meat fillings for variations to this recipe.

1. Combine filling ingredients and set in refrigerator for 1 hour.

2. In a large pot, combine wheat starch, tapioca starch and salt. Make a well in center and pour in rapid boiling water. Stir to moisten ingredients. Cover pot and allow dough to rest 10 minutes.

3. Knead warm dough adding 2t oil until smooth. Keep covered until ready to use.

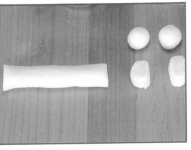

4. Roll dough into a rod and cut into walnut size pieces. Roll each piece in hand until smooth.

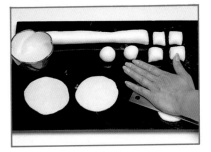

5. Generously oil cleaver and counter top. Press out dough to form a 4″ (10 cm) circle. Center 1T filling and close to form a crescent.

6. Place on oiled steaming plate and steam for 20 minutes. Serve with soy sauce mixed with hot mustard sauce.

35

SHIRIMP DUMPLINGS

One of the most popular dim sum items on a menu.

⟨INGREDIENTS: 3~4 servings⟩

Filling

³/₄ lb (340g)	shrimp shelled, deveined and chopped
¹/₄ C	chopped bamboo shoots
1 t	salt
1 t	sesame seed oil
¹/₂ t	sugar
1	egg white
2 T	cornstarch

Combine filling ingredients and set in refrigerator for 1 hour.

Dough

1 C	wheat starch
¹/₂ C	tapioca starch
¹/₂ t	salt
1 C	boiling water
2 T	oil

NOTE

Dough can be made ahead. Wrap with foil or plastic wrap. Dough keeps one day at room temperature.

1. Mix wheat starch, tapioca starch and salt together in a large pot. Make a well in center and pour in boiling water.

2. Stir to moisten ingredients.

3. Cover pot and allow to rest 10 minutes.

4. Knead until a smooth dough forms, adding oil. Set aside. Keep covered until use.

5. Roll portions of dough into a long roll and cut into walnut size pieces. Roll each piece in hand until smooth. Then generously oil cleaver and counter top. Press out dough to form a 3″ (8cm) circle. (Or use a tortilla press.)

6. Pleat half of circle to form a pouch. Put in 2t filling, cover and pinch ends together.

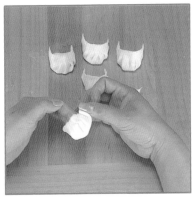

7. Gently curve dumpling to form a crescent.

8. Place on oiled steaming plate and steam 15 minutes.

POT STICKERS

鍋貼

½ pkg Siu Mai wrappers (8 oz, 225 g pkg contains about 80 wrappers).

Filling

1 lb (450g)	ground pork
2 C	chopped nappa
¼ C	chopped onions
1 T	chopped ginger root
1 t	soy sauce
1 t	salt
2 t	sesame seed oil
1 t	wine
½ t	sugar
2 T	cornstarch
3 C	oil for frying
3 C	chicken soup stock

Very easy to prepare. Serve with a dip.

1. Combine filling ingredients.

2. Place 2t filling in center of wrapper, wet edge and seal to form a half circle.

3. Hold top edge and press down to flatten bottom.

4. Heat a 12″ (30 cm) skillet with small amount of oil and fry pot stickers on medium high heat until brown on all sides.

5. Pour ½C soup stock, cover and cook until liquid is absorbed. Serve with soy sauce or vinegar dip, or hot sesame seed oil.

SPRING ROLLS

Delicious with a sweet and sour sauce.

⟨INGREDIENTS: Makes 10 rolls⟩

10   Spring Roll wrappers
2 T oil

Filling
2 C chopped chicken
1   Chinese sausage, chopped
2 T chopped onion
1 C bean sprouts
1   black mushroom, soaked, rinsed and chopped

1/4 C chopped bamboo shoots
2 T soy sauce
1 T rice wine
1/2 t salt
1/2 t sugar
1 T sesame seed oil

Egg white to seal
4 C oil for deep-frying (350°F, 175°C)

1. Combine all filling ingredients. Heat wok and add oil. Stir-fry ingredients and seasonings. Cook for 1/2 minute and try to reduce sauce. If some sauce remains, strain liquid. Filling should not drip.

2. Separate wrappers and wrap filling.

3. Deep-fry for 3 minutes or until golden brown. Serve with sweet and sour sauce or favorite dip.

EGG ROLLS

A favorite side dish for any meal.

⟨INGREDIENTS: Makes 10 ~ 12 rolls⟩

Egg roll skins (10 ~ 12 skins)
2 T   cornstarch dissolved in ¼ C water
4   eggs
½ t   salt
Some oil

Egg roll filling
1 C   lean pork sliced thin
2T   oil
½ C   chopped onions
1 C   beansprouts
½ C   chopped celery
¼ C   chopped bamboo shoots
2 T   chopped water chestnuts

2   large forest mushrooms sliced (soaked until soft and rinsed)
½ t   salt or to taste
1 T   oyster sauce
½ C   water or soup stock
Some cornstarch for thickening

Batter
½ C   flour
¼ C   cornstarch
1 t   baking powder
½ t   baking soda
¾ C   cold water

3 C   oil for deep-frying (375°F, 190°C)

NOTE

If store-bought wrappers must be used, try to use the thinner wrappers available. Store-bought egg roll wrappers need not be dipped into batter before deep-frying.

1. Combine cornstarch mixture, eggs and salt, beat until well blended. Pour a small amount of oil into an 8″ (20 cm) teflon or non-stick frying pan. Rub oil in with a paper towel. Reserve paper towel. Heat skillet on medium heat until hot.

2. Pour small amount of egg mixture into skillet and coat bottom of pan with egg mixture. Quickly pour excess out, back into bowl. Cook until edge pulls from sides of pan. Remove from the pan and set aside. Continue until all of egg mixture is used, oiling the skillet as needed.

3. Heat oil in wok until hot. Add pork and cook until all pink is gone (2 minutes.)

4. Add all other ingredients except cornstarch.

5. Cover, bring to a boil, cook ½ minute.

6. Thicken with cornstarch and water to form a fairly thick sauce. Set aside and allow to cool. Refrigerate until ready to use.

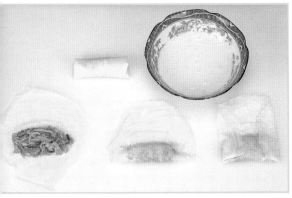

7. Place about 3T filling on the lower bottom of round wrapper. If using square wrappers, place like a diamond in front of you. Bring bottom up to cover filling and roll once. Fold sides in to overlap. Place a small amount of batter at top of wrapper to seal. Continue to roll wrapper until closed. (If no batter is available, mix small amount of flour with water to use as seal.) Mix batter ingredients.

8. Heat 3C oil in wok to 375°F (190°C). Dip each egg roll into batter and deep-fry for 2 minutes, or until golden brown. Turn egg rolls as soon as possible to keep top from breaking open. Continue turning to fry evenly. Continue to fry remaining egg rolls in the same manner. If oil gets too hot, turn to medium high. Always try to maintain 375°F (190°C).

CHICKEN ROLLS

A great tasting appetizer.

⟨INGREDIENTS: Makes 24 rolls⟩

Filling

2	large black forest mushrooms	
1 C	chicken breast	
½ C	bamboo shoots	
½ C	onions	
2 T	oil	
2 T	oyster sauce	
¼ t	salt	

8 sheets phyllo (p 24)
¼ C oil

NOTE

*Phyllo is a tissue thin Mid-Eastern pastry dough, made of flour, eg.
and water. Usually comes in 1 lb (450g) boxes, containing about 2
sheets rolled up. Check edges to be sure of freshness, should b
smooth, not crumbly. To keep from drying during wrapping, sprea
damp towel on counter. Place a sheet of waxed paper over towe
put phyllo sheets on top, cover with another sheet of waxed pape
and damp towel. Make sure phyllo sheets are not directly touchin
damp towel.*

1. Soak mushrooms to soften and rinse. Slice chicken, mushrooms, bamboo shoots, and onions into thin strips. Heat oil in wok and cook chicken until meat turns white. Then add mushrooms, bamboo shoots, and onions, cook ½ minute.

2. Add oyster sauce and salt. Mix thoroughly and remove. Allow mixture to cool before wrapping.

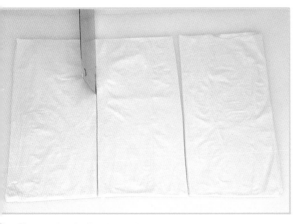

3. Cut each phyllo sheet into thirds.

4. Take one piece and brush half of sheet with oil, fold in half to form a square. Brush with more oil.

5. Place 1T filling in lower corner. Fold corner up to cover filling, then roll up once, fold both sides in to overlap, continue rolling up. Brush entire surface with oil.

6. Place on cookie sheet and bake at 400°F (205°C) for 15 minutes or until golden brown.

CURRY PORK TURNOVERS

A special recipe for a delicious dim sum lunch.

⟨INGREDIENTS: Makes 24⟩

Filling

1 T	oil
1/2 lb (225 g)	ground beef or pork
1/2 C	chopped onions
1/2 C	chopped bamboo shoots
1~2 t	curry powder
3/4 t	salt
1/4 t	sugar
1 T	catsup
8	sheets of phyllo pastry 13 × 17″ (33 × 43cm)
1/2 C	oil

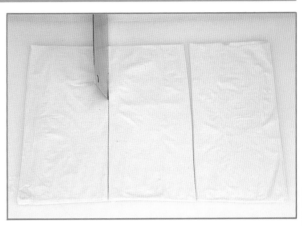

1. Heat 1T oil in wok, brown meat, drain off excess fat. Add all other ingredients and mix together and cook 2 minutes. Remove and allow to cool.

2. Cut phyllo sheets into thirds lengthwise and stack. Keep moist by covering with waxed paper and damp towel.

3. Take one strip, brush half of strip with oil and fold in half lengthwise.

4. Brush top surface with oil and place 1T filling (heaping) on bottom of strip. Fold strip over filling so bottom of strip meets left side. Continue folding at right angles. Tuck at top to form triangle. Brush top and bottom of triangle with oil. Repeat until all dough and filling is used.

NOTE

Phyllo is a tissue thin Mid-Eastern pastry dough, made of flour, egg and water. Usually comes in 1 lb (450g) boxes, containing about 20 sheets rolled up. Check edges to be sure of freshness, should be smooth, not crumbly. To keep from drying during wrapping, spread damp towel on counter. Place a sheet of waxed paper over towel, put phyllo sheets on top, cover with another sheet of waxed paper and damp towel. Make sure phyllo sheets are not directly touching damp towel.

5. Place on cookie sheet and bake at 400°F (205°C) for 15 minutes or until golden brown. (Also may be fried in oil until golden brown.)

FRIED WON TON

An easy, make-ahead party special.

⟨INGREDIENTS: Makes 50⟩

1 lb (450g)   Won Ton wrappers

Filling

$^1/_2$ lb (225g)	ground pork
$^1/_4$ C	chopped onions
1	Chinese sausage, chopped
$^1/_2$ C	chopped bamboo shoots
$^1/_2$ C	chopped green onions
1 t	*mirin* or rice wine
1 t	salt
1 t	soy sauce
2 t	cornstarch
1	egg white
3 C	oil for deep-frying (375°F, 190°C)

Some SWEET AND SOUR SAUCE (p11)

NOTE

Fry ahead and reheat in oven (375°F, 190°C for 5 minutes). Other folding methods can be used. Fold in half sealing edges or fold as in Curry Triangle (p24).

. Combine filling ingredients.

2. Place 1t filling (heaping) on the top corner of wrapper. Fold tip of wrapper over the meat. Roll wrapper until halfway down covering meat. Put a small dab of egg on the left hand side of covered meatball. Pull sides back and pinch together, placing one side on top of the egg white.

3. Fry in oil for 2 minutes until golden brown, turning occasionally. Serve with Sweet and Sour Sauce.

SWEET AND SOUR SAUCE
⟨**INGREDIENTS: Makes 1¹/₂ C**⟩

³/₄ C	water	¹/₂ C	sugar
1¹/₂ T	cornstarch	Dash soy sauce	
¹/₄ C	rice vinegar		
3 T	catsup		

Mix together all ingredients in order. Cook and stir until sauce comes to a full boil. Pour into bowl to use with appetizers.

NOTE
Mix sauce together ahead. Bring to a boil just before serving. Sauce can be kept warm or reheated.

47

SHRIMP AND CREAM CHEESE FRIED WON TONS

Delicious dish served with sweet and sour sauce.

⟨INGREDIENTS: Makes 40⟩

1   12 oz pkg. Won Ton wrappers

Filling

1   8 oz pkg. cream cheese (softened)
$1/2$ C chopped water chestnuts
1 C cooked shrimp meat, chopped
$1/8$ C chopped parsley
$1/2$ t salt
1   egg, beaten
4 C oil for deep-frying

NOTE

Allow cream cheese to stand at room temperature for 1 hour to soften.

1. Place cream cheese in a bowl and allow to soften for 1 hour. Then add remaining filling ingredients.

2. Combine filling ingredients thoroughly.

3. Place 1T of filling in the center of wrapper. Moisten the edges of the wrapper and fold wrapper in the shape of a crescent or triangle, pressing to seal the edges. Continue with remaining wrappers.

4. Heat 4C oil in wok to 325°F (163°C). Deep-fry won tons until golden brown. Remove and drain oil. Serve with your favorite Sweet and Sour sauce.

WOK

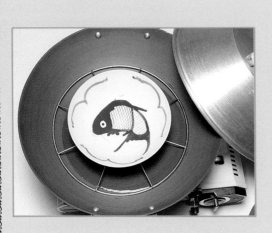

SEASONING THE WOK:

Scrub the wok in hot sudsy water to remove the protective oil applied after manufacturing. Rinse the wok well and dry thoroughly. Then apply a light coat of cooking oil to the inside of the wok with a paper towel and heat it for a few minutes on medium high heat.

Remove the wok, allow it to cool and rinse with hot water. Dry the wok and repeat the above process 2 more times. Now the wok is ready to use.

During the course of cooking a meal, the wok should only be cleaned with hot water. Use a bristle scrub brush to clean the surface, rinse and the wok is ready to cook the next dish.

When finished using the wok, clean and rinse with very hot water. Dry the wok on medium heat to ensure that the surface is completely dry. Then store the wok in a dry place away from steam and moisture to prevent rust. With constant use, your wok will assume a darker color on the inside resulting in a smooth non-stick cooking surface.

FRIED TARO TURNOVERS

Other meat fillings are delicious too.

⟨INGREDIENTS: Makes 10⟩

Filling

1 T	oil	1 lb (450g)	taro root
1 C	ground or diced roast pork	2 T	cornstarch
		½ C	soup stock
¼ C	diced black mushrooms	1 T	oil
		½ t	salt
¼ C	chopped onions	½ C	flour
2 T	oyster sauce	1	egg, beaten
1 t	sesame seed oil	1 C	dehydrated bread crumbs
1 t	five spice powder		
1 T	rice wine	3~4 C	oil for deep-frying (350°F, 175°C)
½ t	salt		
¼ C	soup stock		
1 T	cornstarch		

Use cornstarch to dust fingers

1. Heat wok, add 1T oil. Stir-fry pork until done. Add remaining ingredients. Cook for ½ minute. Dissolve 1T cornstarch in soup and add to pork mixture, bring to a boil to thicken sauce. Remove, set aside and refrigerate.

2. Peel rough skin of taro root, rinse root and slice into ½″ (1.5 cm) thick slices.

3. Arrange in a steamer and steam for ½ hour or until tender.

4. Dissolve 2T cornstarch in ½C soup stock, bring to a boil; cool.

5. Mash taro and mix in enough of thickened soup stock and oil to resemble thick mashed potatoes. Add salt and mix thoroughly.

6. Take about ¼C of the taro mixture, form into a round ball and flatten to form a ½″ (1.5 cm) thick round. Dust your fingers with cornstarch to keep from sticking.

7. Place 1T filling in turnover and close off top; roll in hands to form an oval shape. Coat outside with flour, dip in egg and roll in *panko*.

8. Deep-fry 3~4 minutes or until turnovers are golden brown.

STUFFED *TOFU* TRIANGLES

This recipe can also be steamed.

〈INGREDIENTS: Makes 16〉

2	14 ounce cubes of (*tofu* medium firm)	
1/2 lb(225g)	boneless white fish fillet (approx. 1C)	
1/4 lb(115g)	shrimp, shelled and deveined	
1/2 t	salt	
2 t	rice wine	
1/4 t	white pepper	
1 t	light soy sauce	
1 t	sesame seed oil	
1 t	cornstarch	
1/2	egg white	

2 T slivered ginger root
Fresh Chinese parsley sprigs for garnish

Sauce

1 C rich chicken stock
2 T cornstarch
1 T rice wine
2 T oyster sauce
1 t sesame seed oil
1/4 t sugar

1. Rinse *tofu* cubes and place on a plate and allow to drain off excess liquid for several hours. This is essential to keep oil-spattering to a minimum.

2. Finely mince fish and shrimp until it resembles a paste.

3. Combine with seasoning ingredients. Cut-well drained *tofu* cube into 2 pieces diagonally.

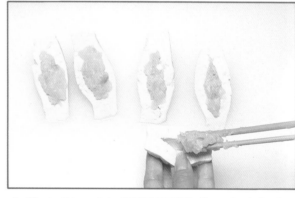

4. Cut each half into 4 equal triangles. Make a slit down the center of each triangle to receive the filling. Open pocket and spoon in 1T filling. Press firmly but gently to mound the filling into and over the top of *tofu*. Repeat until all triangles are filled.

5. Heat oil in wok to 350°F (175°C). Deep-fry *tofu* triangles until light brown (approx. 2 minutes). These are not thoroughly cooked, they must be steamed after this step to completely cook. They must be fried for a further 4 minutes lowering the temperature.

6. Remove *tofu* triangles to individual small plates (2 per plate). Combine sauce ingredients and bring to a full boil stirring constantly. Pour 2T sauce over each plate of *tofu*, garnish with ginger slivers.

7. Place in steamer and cook for 10 minutes just before serving; top with fresh Chinese parsley.

ICED GEODUCK CLAM WITH CILANTRO SAUCE

This dish is delicious when served hot.

⟨INGREDIENTS: 4 ~ 6 servings⟩

1	Geoduck, cleaned, using neck portion only
Large pot of boiling water	
1	green onion
3 ~ 4	slices fresh ginger root
1/4 C	rice wine
1/2 C	sliced red pepper or combination of green and red pepper
2 T	slivered fresh ginger root
1	green onion sliced diagonally

Cilantro Sauce

1/4 C	soy sauce
1/4 C	rice vinegar
2 T	sugar
1 t	minced ginger roo
1	clove garlic, mince
2 T	sesame seed oil
1/4 C	chopped cilantro

. Place geoduck in the sink and pour hot water on the neck of the clam until the skin separates from the neck. Run a knife around inside of the shell to open the clam.

2. Discard stomach and pull off neck.

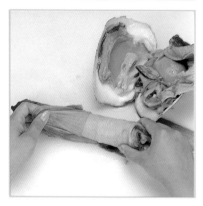

3. Rinse carefully to remove sand and skin.

. Cut off the very tip of the neck and slice open lengthwise.

5. Make incisions lengthwise.

6. Slice into thin pieces.

7. Bring a large pot of water to a boil and add green onion, ginger and wine.

8. Quickly put geoduck slices into boiling water, stir and remove. Blanch in ice water to cool and remove immediately. Drain and lay over a plate of ice.

9. Prepare all vegetables and sprinkle on top of sliced geoduck. Combine ingredients for sauce and serve as a dip.

SKEWERED SHRIMP WITH PEPPERS 青椒蝦串

Delicious made with scallops.

⟨INGREDIENTS: 4 servings⟩

1 lb (450g)	shelled and deveined shrimp
1/2 C	Plum Sauce or favorite barbecue sauce
1	small green pepper cut into chunks

1. Skewer shrimp and pepper chunks.

2. Baste with plum sauce and broil until shrimp is done. Serve with hot steamed rice.

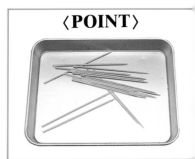

⟨POINT⟩

* If barbecuing over hot coals, be sure to soak bamboo skewers in water for 1 hour before skewering ingredients.

Wonderful as a complete meal.

⟨INGREDIENTS: 4~6 Servings⟩

4 C	green lettuce leaves	**Dressing**
1/4 C	sliced green and red pepper	1/3 C soy sauce
1/4 C	sliced yellow pepper	1/3 C rice vinegar
10	pea pods, strings removed	3 T sesame seed oil
1/4 C	sliced carrots	3 T sugar
1/4 C	sliced water chestnuts	1 t minced garlic
1/4 C	cilantro	1 t minced ginger root
1/2 lb (225g)	cooked prawns	

1. Prepare all vegetables and arrange attractively in a salad dish. Arrange prawns on top of salad greens.

2. Prepare salad dressing and shake to combine thoroughly. Toss salad with dressing just before serving.

CALAMARI WITH HOT BEAN SAUCE

Other shell fish are delicious.

⟨INGREDIENTS: 4 ~ 6 servings⟩

2 lbs (900g)	calamari (squid)
1 T	oil
1	clove garlic, minced
1 t	minced ginger
½ C	each, green and red pepper, sliced
1 T	hot bean paste
2 T	soy sauce
1 T	rice wine
Salt to taste	
1	green onion, chopped
Cilantro	

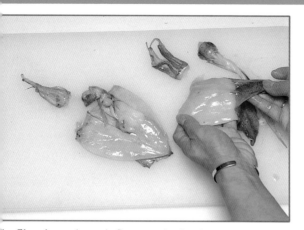

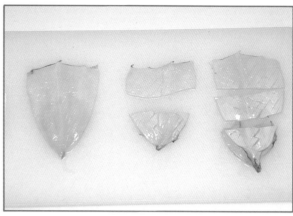

1. Cleaning calamari. Cut open body of calamari; clean. Cut off tentacles and reserve. Remove purple membrane, rinse body and tentacles; drain well.

2. Score the calamari. Cut calamari into 2″ (5 cm) pieces.

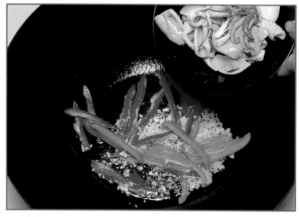

3. Bring a pot of water to a boil, drop in calamari, stir and remove. Drain thoroughly and set aside.

4. Heat wok, add oil and stir-fry garlic and giner. Add peppers and remaining ingredients. Return calamari to wok and combine. Be careful not to overcook calamari.

VEGETABLES

Selection of vegetables is important. Select for the balance of flavor, color and texture.

Cutting: Density and size of vegetable determines cutting style and thickness. This in turn determines the cooking time and tenderness.

Finely shredded vegetables require less cooking time and in turn less liquid to cooking.

Denser vegetables such as broccoli, cauliflower and green beans require more liquid and longer cooking time.

Judy Lew

Serve over pan-fried noodles for a delicious chow mein.

⟨INGREDIENTS: 4~6 servings⟩

½ lb (225g)	seafood, (scallops, prawns or fish or combination)
1	clove garlic, minced
½ t	grated fresh ginger root
1 t	rice wine
1 T	cornstarch
2 t	soy sauce
2 T	oil

2 C	assorted vegetables (eggplant, mushrooms, onions, pea pods, red and green pepper)
2 T	rice wine
½ t	salt
½ C	soup stock
1 T	cornstarch (dissolve in soup stock)

1. Prepare vegetables.

2 Marinate seafood with garlic, ginger root, rice wine, cornstarch and soy sauce.

3. Heat wok and add 2T oil; stir-fry seafood and remove.

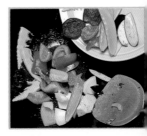

4. Add vegetables to wok, add rice wine, salt and soup stock. Bring to a full boil stirring constantly. Return seafood to wok and cook for ½ minute.

SHRIMP BALLS

Serve as an appetizer.

⟨**INGREDIENTS: Makes 20 balls**⟩

1/2 lb (225g)	shrimp (shelled and deveined)
1/4 lb (115g)	boneless fish fillet
1/2	egg white
2 T	cornstarch
1/2 t	salt
1/8 t	grated fresh ginger root
1/8 t	minced garlic
1/2 t	sugar
1 T	rice wine
2~3 C	oil for deep-frying

1. Finely mince shrimp and fish. Combine thoroughly with remaining ingredients.

2. Shape into 1 1/2" (4 cm) balls. Wet fingers to keep meat from sticking.

3. Deep-fry in 350°F (175°C) oil for 2 minutes. Remove and drain. Serve with soy sauce and hot mustard.

SHRIMP EGG FU YUNG

A quick and easy complete meal.

⟨INGREDIENTS: 4 servings⟩

1 T	oil
1/3 C	sliced onions
1/2 C	sliced fresh mushrooms
1/2 C	chopped chives or other green vegetable thinly sliced
1 C	beansprouts
6	eggs
1 C	cooked shrimp
1/2 t	salt
2~3 T	oil

NOTE

Other cooked meats such as chicken or ham may be used.

1. Prepare all ingredients.

2. Heat 1T oil in wok and stir-fry onions, mushrooms, chives and beansprouts just until limp (about ½ minute). Set aside.

3. Combine the eggs, shrimp, salt and vegetable.

4. Stir gently.

5. Heat a skillet and add 2T oil to coat the bottom of skillet. Add all egg mixture and cook in the same manner as scrambled eggs.

6. Gently stir mixture to cook thoroughly. Serve with oyster sauce.

BONELESS STUFFED CHICKEN WINGS WITH SWEET RICE

Any other stuffings can be used.

⟨**INGREDIENTS: Makes 12**⟩

2 lbs (900g) or 12 chicken wings

¹/₂   quantity Treasured Sweet Rice (p 72)

Marinade

3 T	soy sauce
1 T	sugar
1 T	*mirin*
1 t	chopped garlic
1 t	chopped fresh ginger root

Basting Sauce

1 T	soy sauce
1 T	*mirin*

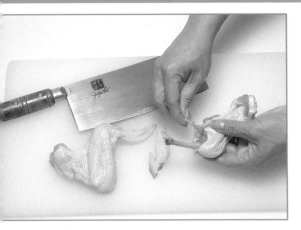

. Remove 2 bones and tip.

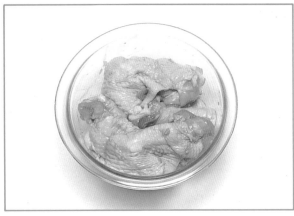

2. Rub boneless chicken wings with marinade and let stand 1 hour.

3. Prepare ½ recipe of Treasured Sweet Rice.

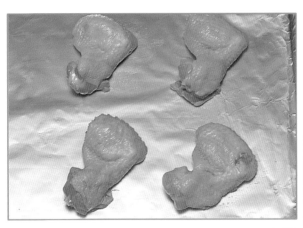

4. If cooking chicken right away, stuff, and roast at 375°F (190°C) for ½ hour.

5. Baste with some sauce during baking for added color.

NOTE

Allow filling to cool and stuff chicken just before baking. Bake for 45 minutes if chicken is very cold.

STEAMED BEEF MEATBALLS 蒸牛肉丸子

Steaming retains the flavor of the meat and this dish is easy to make.

⟨INGREDIENTS: 4～6 servings⟩

1 lb(450g)	lean ground beef	1/2 t	salt
2 T	finely chopped water chestnuts	1 T	soy sauce
		1 T	sesame seed oil
2 T	finely chopped onions	1/2 t	white pepper
1	clove garlic, chopped	1/2 t	sugar
2 T	chopped Chinese black mushrooms	1 T	cornstarch
		1	egg white
1/4 C	chopped green onions		

Optional Dips

Hoisin sauce, hot mustard, plum sauce, or hot sauce.

∗ Wet fingers with water to keep mixture from sticking.

1. Combine all ingredients thoroughly.

2. Stir meat one way.

3. Shape into 2″ (5cm) meatballs.

4. Place in small plates and steam for 20 minutes. Serve with your favorite sauce or dip.

An easy appetizer to serve for parties.

⟨INGREDIENTS: Makes 25⟩

1 lb (450g)	tender beef steak sliced into bacon size thin strips
25	chunks green pepper or mushrooms
25	chunks pineapple
Sauce	
¼ C	soy sauce
2 T	sugar
2 T	*mirin*
2	cloves garlic, crushed
1 t	grated fresh ginger root

1. Marinate beef in sauce for ½ hour. Roll strip of beef into a ball and place on skewer alternating with green pepper, another beef strip and top with a pineapple chunk.

2. Place kabobs on broiling pan and bake 10 minutes at 425°F (220°C).

3. Delicious served with hot steamed rice as a main course. If barbecuing over hot coals, be sure to soak bamboo skewers in water for 1 hour before placing food on (see page 56).

PORK WITH SCRAMBLED EGGS

Delicious when served with Chinese mandarin pancakes.

〈INGREDIENTS: 4 servings〉

1/2 C	sliced forest mushrooms
1/2 C	tiger lily buds
1/4 C	cloud ears
1/2 C	bamboo shoots, sliced
3	eggs
1/2 t	salt
1 T	oil
2 T	oil
1/2 lb (225g)	boneless pork, sliced thin
2 T	*mirin*
1 t	soy sauce
1/4 C	soup stock
2	green onions, chopped
1	head lettuce*

* For a spicy taste, add
1t of hot bean paste.
*Use carrots for added
color.

* Separate the head of lettuce, using small leaves as cups, and place on a platter.

68

. Soak mushrooms, tiger lily buds, and cloud ears until
oft (10 minutes). Wash well and slice thin. Set aside.

2. Beat eggs, adding salt. Fry in 1T oil in the wok to make
scrambled eggs and set aside.

. Add 2T oil to wok and cook pork on high heat 2
ninutes.

4. Add mushrooms, tiger lily buds, cloud ears, bamboo
shoots, carrots, *mirin* and soy sauce. Stir together, adding
soup stock. Cover, bring to a boil and cook 1 minute.

. Add green onions and mix in eggs, breaking into small
ieces. Serve with lettuce cup or steamed white rice.

STEAMED GLUTINOUS RICE

⟨INGREDIENTS:
Makes 4 cups⟩

2 C glutinous rice

1. Rinse rice until water runs clear. Allow rice to soak in water for 2 hours; drain.

2. Place a cloth in a steaming rack spread rice out to an even layer. Make hole in center of rice. Cover steamer bring water to a full boil and reduce temperature to medium high. Steam for 4(minutes.

NOTE
Rice is an integral part of every meal, and is the staple food of China. Basically, there are three types: long grain, short grain, and glutinous, or sweet rice. Long grain rice is firmer, and is used for fried rice. Short grain is starchier and softer. Japanese sushi requires use of short grain rice. Sweet rice is usually used for desserts or stuffings.

Serve with any mea

STEAMED WHITE RICE

⟨**INGREDIENTS**⟩

yields 3 cups	yields 4 cups
1 C rice (long grain)	1½ C rice (short grain)
1½ C water	1¾ C water

∗ Water proportion changes as more rice is used. If cooking more rice, add enough water to cover rice 1″ (1.5 cm) or water level should be up to first joint of index finger. Increase or decrease water to the firmness desired.

∗ When cooking short grain rice, use a little less water.

∗ Leftover rice may be refrigerated. Reheat by steaming or use for fried rice.

1. Wash rice by rubbing between hands. (Some brands require no wahsing.) Drain and repeat until water is clear.

2. Add water, cover saucepan an bring to a boil.

3. When rice comes to a boil, uncover and allow to boil until 75% or most of liquid evaporates and holes form on surface of rice. Cover rice, allow to steam on very low heat for 20 minutes.

4. Turn heat off and allow rice to sit 5 minutes on burner.

5. Fluff rice before serving.

PEARL BALLS 珍珠丸子

An easy menu for dim sum buffet.

⟨INGREDIENTS: Makes 18⟩

Meat Mixture

1 lb(450g)	lean ground pork
1	Chinese sausage, minced
1/4 C	chopped bamboo shoots
	Chinese mushroom, soaked, rinsed and chopped
1 T	rice wine
1 T	soy sauce
1 t	salt

2 T	cornstarch
1 T	sesame seed oil
5	water chestnuts cut into quarters
1 C	sweet rice (soaked in water for 1 hour and drained)

NOTE

Food coloring can be added to soaking rice to obtain different colors.

1. Combine meat mixture. Surround each piece of water chestnut with meat mixture to form a 1½″ (4 cm) ball. Roll each meat ball in sweet rice.

2. Place in a steamer and steam for 25 minutes.

TREASURED SWEET RICE 糯米飯

〈INGREDIENTS: 4 servings〉

2 C   cooked Glutinous ri
      (p 70)

1 T   oil
1   Chinese sausage, dice
1 C   diced barbecued pork
1/2 C diced Chinese black mus
      rooms
Seasonings
2 T   soy sauce
1 T   rice wine
1 T   sesame seed oil
1 T   oyster sauce
1/2 t sugar
1/8 t white pepper

A delicious stuffing for chicken.

1. Prepare mushrooms and sausage. Heat wok, and oil, Barbecued Pork, Chinese sausage, and mushrooms.

2. Add seasoning mixture and stir in rice, combinin thoroughly. Place in individual serving bowls place i steamer and steam for 15 minutes (Can be made ahea and steamed just before serving).

–APPLICATION– A delicacy wrapped in the packag

〈INGREDIENTS: Makes 6〉

6	lotus leaves	1 T oil
1/2 lb (225g)	boneless chicken, diced in to 1″ (1.5cm) cubes	1 C diced barbecued pork
		2 Chinese sausages, diced
Marinade for chicken		2 black mushrooms, soaked and diced
1/2 t	grated fresh ginger	2 T soy sauce
2 t	soy sauce	3 T oyster sauce
2 t	sesame seed oil	
1/2 t	sugar	2 hard boiled eggs, quartered
1 T	cornstarch	1/2 C Chinese parsley
4 C	STEAMED GLUTINOUS RICE (p 70) or mixture of long grain and short grain rice	

. Soak lotus leaves in hot water and thoroughly rinse. Pat dry.

2. Combine chicken with marinade, set aside. Have rice hot and ready. Heat wok, add oil and stir-fry chicken until meat is white. Add pork, sausage, mushrooms, soy sauce and oyster sauce.

3. Turn off heat and thoroughly mix in rice. Divide rice into 6 equal portions.

. Place ¹/₂ of portion of rice on top ide of leaf. Put 1 piece of egg in enter and cover with parsley.

5. Cover with remaining portion of rice.

6. Fold bottom of leaf up to cover rice, bring in sides and roll up to enclose contents.

Continue with other packets.

Place wrapped rice in steamer and eam for 20 minutes.

RICE WRAPPED IN LOTUS LEAF

荷葉飯

NOTE

Larger packets can be made if desired adjusting steaming time.

73

CONGEE

Good recipe for any time.

⟨INGREDIENTS: 4 servings⟩

1 C	calrose rice	Soy sauce
8 C	seasoned soup stock	White pepper
		Thinly sliced fresh ginger root

Side ingredients and condiments

Chopped cooked ham
Sesame seed oil
Cilantro

8	shrimp, shelled, deveined and sliced in half
1/4 lb (115g)	boneless white fish fillet, sliced into 1/4″ (1 cm)
4	eggs (optional)
1/8 C	chopped salted turnips

NOTE

Place condiments in small dish and allow each person to sele their own adding it directly *their own bowl of CONGEE*

. Rinse rice 2 or 3 times.

2. Add seasoned soup stock and bring to a slow simmer.

3. Simmer for 2 hours slowly, until the texture is smooth.

. Prepare all other ingredients while CONGEE is simmering.

5. Add fish and shrimp, simmer for 1 minute. Serve CONGEE with assorted desired condiments. Place in bottom of bowl and pour hot CONGEE into bowl.

BASIC CHICKEN STOCK
INGREDIENTS: Makes 6C ⟩

chicken or 3C bones
C water
slices fresh ginger root
scallion

1. Place the chicken or bones, ginger, scallion and the water in a pot and bring to a full boil on high heat. Skim froth and fat, turn temperature to simmer, cover and simmer stock for 1 hour or until chicken is cooked.

2. Remove chicken or bones and strain soup stock with a fine mesh strainer. Cheese cloth may be used if desired. Skim soup of excess fat. Allow soup to cool, then refrigerate. Fat will harden on the surface and can be easily removed with a strainer.

Any meat or vegetable can be used.

⟨**INGREDIENTS: WHEAT STARCH DOUGH**⟩

1 C wheat starch	1 C boiling water
½ C tapioca starch	½ T oil
½ t salt	

NOTE

Measure 1C water and bring to a rapid boil. Water must be boiling for dough to form properly.

1. Combine wheat starch, tapioca starch and salt in a large bowl. Make a well in the center and pour in rapidly boiling water.

2. Stir to moisten ingredients, cover bowl and allow to stand 5 minutes.

3. Knead dough to form a ball and turn out onto a clean surface. Knead dough until smooth, cover until ready to use.

〈INGREDIENTS: 4~6 servings〉

1	recipe silver pin noodles (p 76)	¼ C	sliced mushrooms
¼ lb (115g)	boneless chicken, thinly sliced	¼ C	sliced red pepper
		¼ C	sliced green pepper
1	clove garlic, minced	½ C	beansprouts
1 T	soy sauce	1	green onion, sliced
1 t	sugar	2 T	soy sauce
1 t	cornstarch	2 t	sesame seed oil
3 T	oil	1 T	rice wine
½ C	sliced onions	¼ t	white pepper

1. Prepare 1 recipe of wheat starch dough. Divide dough into 2 equal portions. Divide each into ½″ (1.5 cm) balls and roll between palms of hand to form a pin-shaped noodle.

2. Place noodles on an oiled steaming plate and steam for 5 minutes. Remove and set aside to use as noodles.

3. Marinate chicken with garlic, soy sauce, sugar and cornstarch. Prepare all other ingredients.

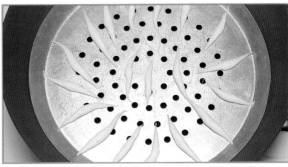

4. Heat wok, add oil. When oil is hot, add chicken and cook until done. Add all vegetables and stir-fry for ½ minute.

THICKENING

Cornstarch and water is the most popular mixture used to thicken a sauce. Dissolve 1T of cornstarch in 2T of water. Use as needed to thicken sauce to the desired consistency. Always bring sauce to a full boil and then thoroughly combine ingredients together.

FRESHEST INGREDIENTS OF THE SEASON, ATTENTION TO THE TECHNIQUE OF STIR-FRYING, COOKING JUST UNTIL CRISP AND TENDER AND MOST IMPORTANTLY BE CNSISTENT AND ORGANIZED.

5. Add noodles and all other ingredients. Continue to stir-fry until noodles are hot and all ingredients are combined.

CHOW FOON

An all time favorite for dim sum lunch.

STEAMED NOODLES

〈INGREDIENTS: Makes 5～6 rolls〉

1 C	cake flour, sifted
2 T	cornstarch
1/2 t	salt
1 T	oil
1 1/4 C	water

1. Combine all ingredients thoroughly, making sure there are no lumps. Use a blender if preferred. Strain mixture if lumps are present. Prepare the wok for steaming with a rack to hold an 8″ or 9″ (20 or 23 cm) round cake pan.

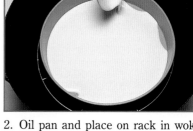

2. Oil pan and place on rack in wok. Pour in about 1/3C of batter just to cover bottom of pan.

3. Cover, and steam on high heat for 5 minutes. Remove pan from steamer and float pan in some cold water. Allow to cool.

4. Remove noodle from pan by rolling (jelly roll style). Clean pan if necessary and repeat process until all batter is used. Use several pans to make this process easier and faster.

⟨INGREDIENTS: 4～6 servings⟩

½ lb (225g)	rice noodles (to soften noodles, steam or microwave)
3 T	oil
¼ lb (115g)	sliced boneless chicken
¼ lb (115g)	shrimp, shelled and deveined
½ C	pea pods
½ C	sliced green or red peppers
¼ C	sliced mushrooms

1 C	beansprouts
1	green onion sliced
1 T	oyster sauce
2 T	soy sauce
2 T	rice wine
¼ t	salt
1 T	sesame seed oil

Cilantro for garnish

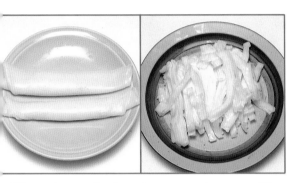

. Warm rice noodles in a steamer or microwave. Slice noodles into wide pieces.

2. Cut up chicken pieces.

. Prepare all remaining ingredients.

4. Heat wok and add oil. Stir-fry meat until done, push up to sides of wok.

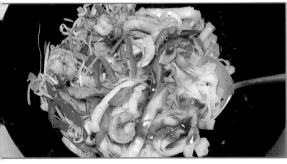

. Add all vegetables and seasoning ingredients with the noodles. Combine gently and transfer to a plate. Garnish with cilantro.

CURRY MAIFUN NOODLES

An easy alternative to chow mein.

⟨INGREDIENTS: 4~6 servings⟩

4 oz	dried rice noodles (maifun)
2 T	oil
1/2 lb (225g)	boneless chicken, sliced thin
1/2 C	sliced onions
1 C	beansprouts
1/2 C	sliced mushrooms
1/2 C	sliced green and red peppers
8	pea pods
1	green onion sliced

Seasoning

1 T	curry powder to taste
1 T	oyster sauce
2 T	soy sauce
1 T	sesame seed oil
1 t	sugar
2 T	rice wine or chicken stock

. Soak maifun in warm water until soft (approx. ½ our). Drain and set aside.

2. Cut up chicken pieces.

. Prepare all remaining ingredients.

4. Heat wok and add oil, stir-fry chicken until done. Add all vegetables, stir to combine.

. Add maifun and all seasoning ingredients. Combine horoughly turning down the temperature if necessary. ook for 1 minute or until all ingredients are hot.

Quick and Easy sweets to make. Other sweet fillings can be used.

⟨**INGREDIENTS: Makes 40**⟩

Banana Filling

3	bananas cut into ¼″ (1.5 cm) slices
3 T	sugar
¼ t	cinnamon
3 C	oil for deep frying
¼ C	powdered sugar

1. Combine all ingredients and use as a filling for won ton wrappers.

2. Fill with banana filling and seal with water.

3. Deep-fry in 325°F (163°C) oil until light brown.

4. Remove from oil and dust with powdered sugar if desired.

⟨INGREDIENTS: Makes 40⟩

Apple Filling
3 C peeled, sliced apples
2 T sugar (use less sugar if apples are sweet)
¼ t cinnamon
½ C raisins
3 C oil for deep-frying
¼ C powdered sugar

Peel apples and slice into small pieces.

2. Combine all ingredients and use as a filling for won ton wrappers.

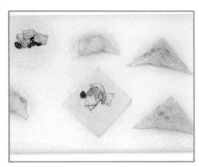

3. Fill with apple filling and seal with water to form a triangle.

Deep-fry in 325°F (163°C) oil until light brown.

5. Remove from oil and dust with powderd sugar if desired.

Tea

Tea is the traditional drink served immediately before and after a Chinese meal. The choice of tea is entirely up to individual tastes. There are basically three groups of teas.

Greentea—Unfermented, dried in the sun. Delicate flavor and light in color.

Oolong tea—Partially fermented green tea imparting a slightly stronger flavor.

Red or Black tea—Fermented tea which are first dried in the sun and then over charcoal. They possess the strongest flavor among the three varieties of tea.

The scented teas of which jasmine tea is by far the most popular, are made mostly from partially fermented tea.

Tea is properly brewed in porcelain pots and cups. Clean and heat the teapot by pouring in brisk boiling water and waiting until the teapot is warm before discarding the water. Next, add tea leaves and pour in fresh boiling water. Allow the covered tea to steep for approximately 3 minutes. The tea leaves may be reused for a second or even third brewing, but remember to leave some tea in the pot for the next brewing in order for the tea to release its full aroma.

EGG CUSTARD TARTS

A very delicious dessert.

⟨INGREDIENTS: 18~20 tarts⟩

Custard		Pastry	
1¼ C	hot water	1½ C	all purpose flour sifted
½ C	sugar	1 T	sugar
4	eggs	½ C	chilled butter
1 t	vanilla	2 T	shortening
1 t	vinegar	1	egg
		1 t	vanilla

1. Dissolve sugar in hot water, allow cool and add remaining ingredients.

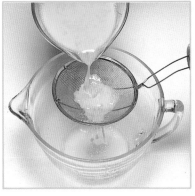

2. Strain egg mixture. Set aside.

3. Combine flour with sugar. Cut in butter and shortening until mixture resembles coarse meal.

4. Combine egg with vanilla and add flour mixture.

5. Mix well.

6. Turn dough onto a lightly floured surface and knead for 30 seconds.

7. Divide dough into 18 pieces and press into 2½″ (6.5 cm) tart pans. Press to ¼″ (1 cm) thickness, fluting edge. Arrange tart shells 1″ (2.5 cm) apart on baking sheet. Stir custard mixture, pour into each shell. Bake at 375°F (190°C) for 20 minutes. Serve hot or cool.

STEAMED TARO CAKE

This delightful dish can be reheated by pan-frying.

⟨INGREDIENTS: 4~6 servings⟩

Meat Filling

1 T	oil
¼ lb(115g)	boneless pork cut into ½″ (1.5cm) dices
2	Chinese sausages diced
¼ C	diced ham
2 T	chopped salted turnip
½ t	salt
¼ t	five spice powder
1 T	rice wine

1 T	oil
2 C	diced taro root
½ t	salt
½ C	soup stock

Cake Mixture

1 C	cake flour, sifted
¼ C	tapioca starch
1½ C	chicken stock (p7
¼ C	chopped gree onions
1 T	toasted sesam seeds

Heat wok, add 1T oil. Stir-fry pork and sausage until ork turns grey. Add ham, turnip, salt, five spice powder d wine. Stir-fry until sauce reduces, remove contents d set aside.

2. Peel taro, slice and dice. Heat a clean wok and add 1T oil.

Stir-fry taro root adding ½C soup ock. Cover, bring to a boil, reduce mperature to medium high and ok for 5 minutes or until soup stock s reduced. Remove and allow to ol.

4. Combine cake flour, tapioca starch and chicken stock in a bowl. Combine mixture thoroughly making sure there are no lumps.

5. Lightly grease a 9″ (23 cm) round cake pan. Place in 1 layer of taro root. Scatter in meat filling.

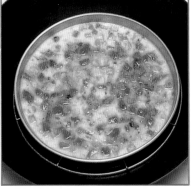

. Cover with cake mixture. Repeat rocess until the pan is full, ending ith a scattering of meat mixture.

7. Steam the mixture in a steamer for ½ hour. When cake is done, scatter with green onions or parsley. Sprinkle on sesame seeds.

8. Allow cake to cool before slicing. Traditionally this cake is sliced in diamond shaped pieces. Start by cutting strips 2″ (5 cm) wide. Then make diagonal slices 2″ (5 cm) wide again.

FORTUNE COOKIES

⟨INGREDIENTS: Makes 25⟩

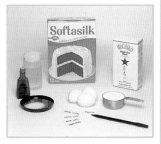

1 C cake flour, sifted
3 T sweet rice flour (or cornstarch)
1/2 C sugar
1/4 t salt
1/4 C vegetable oil
3 egg whites
1/4 C water
1 t vanilla extract

Paper fortunes

Fun recipe for special parties.

1. Combine cake flour, sweet rice flour, sugar and salt in a bowl, set aside.

2. In a large bowl, combine oil, egg whites, water and vanilla. Beat on medium speed for 1 minute. Mix in dry ingredients and blend until smooth.

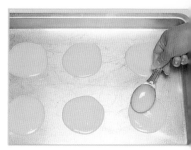

3. Drop 1T batter onto a lightly oile cookie sheet. Spread batter with a spoo in a circular motion to a 4″ (10 cm) roun

NOTE

Bake only a few cookies at a time.

If cookies harden before folding , reheat i oven. Wear cloth gloves if cookies are to hot to handle. For even browning, use dark, heavy cookie sheet.

4. Bake 15 or 20 minutes at 325°F (163°C) or until light brown. Remove cookies one at a time from oven. Place fortune on cookie, fold in half and quickly bend on the edge of a can.

5. Place in a muffin pan to keep cookies in shape.

INFORMATION

Planning The DIM SUM Menu

When planning a dim sum menu, consider the different methods of cooking, texture of eac menu item, flavors and ease of preparation. Many types of dim sum can be prepared ahea and reheated. Dim sum preparation requires considerable hand work, therefore it is easie to include other dishes such as noodles or other stir fry dishes.

In serving a Chinese meal, there is no single main course as in the typical American mea but a combination of courses to be presented simultaneously for everyone to enjoy. The Chines serve two different types of meals depending upon the occasion and circumstances. The forma banquet dinner is appropriate for a larger group of people celebrating a special event whil the more common informal dinner is more of a practical everyday meal. The recipes an emphasis of this book are directed toward the successful preparation of an informal Chines meal and I would strongly suggest mastering the preparation of an informal dinner befor attempting to serve a banquet.

A formal Chinese banquet is served to a gathering of ten or more guests customarily seate around a large round table with a revolving "Lazy Susan" in the center of the table for eas access to individual dinner courses by the guests. The banquet would normally consist o ten courses served in a particular order by a staff of servants. A large platter of cold mea and vegetable appetizers is usually first to arrive. Then followed by two to four stir-fried dishe The banquet always includes a hot soup which may be served at any point in the banque but traditionally near the end of the meal. The premier entrees such as a whole duck o fish would follow the stir-fried dishes. Rice or noodles would then be served to complete th banquet. All the dishes are brought out in quick succession to insure that all courses ar hot and delicious. Finally, tea is served to end the banquet. Wine may also be served throughou the entire meal. The Chinese banquet is very elaborate and as such, should be reserved fo very special occasions.

The informal Chinese dinner is more appropriately suited for the life styles of today. Nutr tious, economical, and easy to prepare, Chinese food is most of all delicious. The informa dinner is designed for a party of four people. In any event, keep the group to less than te people unless you plan to serve a buffet style dinner.

Planning your menu is the important first step in preparing the meal. Always prepare a much in advance as possible so as to be able to enjoy your company instead of being stuc in the kitchen. It is also a good practice to try a recipe before cooking it for guests. Alway read the entire recipe before starting to cook.

The menu chart illustrates sample menus for varying groups of people. For instance, a informal meal for four people would consist of one each of an appetizer, soup, rice or noodl meat of your choice, seafood, and vegetable dish.

Generally, rice always accompanies a Chinese meal. Dessert is usually fresh fruit in seaso and tea is served at the end of the meal.

For every two additional people, i.e., 6, 8, 10, add one meat dish of your choice and increas the vegetable selection by $1/2$ recipe. Rather than increase the recipe, you may prefer to mak wo different vegetable dishes. When in doubt as to how much food to prepare, remember t is far better to have leftovers than to run short of food at the dinner table.

When planning your menu, always consider the balance of flavors, the required ingredients, and cutting/cooking methods previously mentioned. Incorporate different meats and vegetables to vary the menu. For example, cook one dish of chicken, one dish of beef, and one dish of pork instead of three chicken dishes.

However, you may also economize by working the menu around one major roast or meat. By using a pork loin end roast for instance, portions of the roast can be cut for barbecued pork or sweet and sour pork. Bits and pieces of pork may further be used in the making of won ton filling or chow mein. The remaining bones may then be simmered for an excellent soup stock. Even the last bits of cooked pork on the bones can be removed and used in fried rice or egg fu yung. This efficient and economical use of meat also applies to the use of a whole chicken. Whenever possible, balance the menu by serving a different meat dish or use different meats in the vegetable dishes. You can always save what is not used for another meal with the aid of a freezer to preserve your meats.

The greatest assets in Chinese cooking are your resourcefulness, ingenuity, and ability to adapt in the face of unavailable ingredients. Shopping for weekly specials at your grocery store and preparing your menu accordingly will save you money. Of course, you may always choose to increase a recipe rather than prepare two separate recipes which will necessitate a shorter list of required ingredients.

MENU CHART

Number of People Served:	2	4	6	8	10
Course					
APPETIZER	*	*	*	*	*
SOUP	*	*	*	*	*
RICE	*	*	*	*	*
(Allow ½ Cup uncooked or 1½ Cups cooked rice per person)					
MEAT-BEEF	1	1	1	1	1
-CHICKEN			1	1	1
-PORK				1	1
(Selection of beef, chicken, or pork dish is up to you)					
SEAFOOD		1	1	1	1
VEGETABLE	1	1	1½	2	2½ or 3
DESSERT	*	*	*	*	*
(Usually fresh fruit)					

* ADJUST RECIPE FOR NUMBER OF PEOPLE.

COOKING METHODS

The most common Chinese cooking methods include stir-frying, deep-frying, roasting, an
steaming. Depending upon the method utilized, ingredients generally retain their natural flavo
and nutrition with new and different tastes emerging from the use of each method.

Stir-Frying

This method of cooking combines the elements of high heat and quick, constant tossing to seal i
the flavor and juices of meats and vegetables. Stir-frying cooks protein foods thoroughly at the sam
time leaving them tender and juicy. Vegetables stir-fried until barely tender retain their natural colo
and crisp texture.

Only a small amount of oil is necessary. Timing and temperature will vary according to the type o
pan selected and whether a gas or electric range is used. A flat-bottomed pan or wok which has con
tact with the heating element will get much hotter than a round-bottomed one. In addition, a ga
range is more convenient since you can turn the heat up or down instantly. A good stir-frying tempe
ature is 375°F (190°C). If the temperature is too high, the food will burn in which case a lowe
temperature adjustment is in order. On the other hand, if the temperature is too low, ingredients d
not fry, but seep in the oil and will lose their flavor. Therefore, to maintain the proper temperature
constant adjustment of the temperature may be necessary.

Actual stir-frying involves vigorous arm action in the constant stirring and tossing of the food. It i
a loud and noisy operation when the food meets the pan and the stirring begins. Actual cooking tim
will seldom exceed several minutes.

Follow the steps below for effective stir-frying:

1) Heat the wok until it barely gets hot and add oil (usually 2T).
2) Roll the oil around to cover the cooking surface of the wok.
3) When the oil begins to form a light haze, yo are ready to add the ingredients.
4) Follow the recipe and remember to adjust th temperature control for the proper stir-fryin temperature.

Cornstarch for Thickening

Sauces or gravies can be thickened with a variety of starches such as arrowroot, potato, tapioca, o
cornstarch. All of these starches produce a translucent gravy, whereas flour will produce an opaqu
gravy. In Chinese cooking, cornstarch is most often used.

Many recipes call for cornstarch for thickening, but sometimes an exact amount is not given. Mi
equal amounts of cornstarch to cold water and stir until cornstarch is dissolved. Usually 1 T cornstarc
dissolved in 1 T cold water will be enough to thicken ½ C sauce to produce a medium thick grav
To thicken a sauce, always push all ingredients to the side of the wok, making a well at the bottor
of the wok. Stir cornstarch mixture and pour a small amount into the well. Stir the sauce constantl
to prevent lumps. Allow the sauce to come to a boil and see how thick it is. If not thick enough, ad
more cornstarch mixture until desired thickness is obtained. Always remember to stir the sauce con
stantly to prevent lumps from forming. When desired thickness is obtained, mix ingredients togethe
gently to coat with sauce.

Deep-Frying

Deep-frying requires a large amount of oil in the wok, usually not more than 3–4 C. A 14 inch (35 cn
wok is best suited for deep-frying. As with stir-frying, timing and temperature for deep-frying wi
vary depending upon whether a gas or electric stove is used. Thus, the time given for most recipe
is only approximate and adjustments should be made accordingly. Added caution should be exercise
whenever oil is used at high temperatures. Never leave the hot oil unattended!

The proper temperature for deep-frying is generally 375°F (190°C). The oil should reach this tempera
ture before any ingredients are added. At a temperature of 375°F (190°C) the oil will just barely begi
to smoke. An easy way to tell whether the oil has reached the desired temperature is to add a dro
of batter into the oil. If the drop of batter sinks and slowly returns to the surface, the oil is not ye
hot enough. If the batter drops to the bottom and immediately bounces up to the surface, the oil i
ready for deep-frying. If the oil smokes, it has gotten too hot and the temperature should be lowered
The oil used for deep-frying can be saved and used again. To grant your oil longer life, remove foo

rumbs with the fine mesh strainer during deep-frying. The quality of used oil is judged by its clarity, ot by the number of times used nor the length of time used. Fresh oil is light yellow in color and lear. If the used oil is still relatively clear, it is salvageable and readily usable again. However, used il which appears darker and clouded should be discarded because the temperature at which it will egin to smoke will drop and consequently, a high enough temperature cannot be achieved for proper eep-frying resulting in foods turning out very greasy.

o store the used oil, first strain with a fine mesh strainer. Then place the oil in a heatproof container the oil is still hot. Allow the oil to cool, cover, and store in the refrigerator until ready to use again. eanut oil or good vegetable oil such as corn oil will have a longer usable life as well as possess quali- es superior to other oils for purposes of deep-frying foods. None of the pure vegetable oils contain holesterol and the use of a polyunsaturated oil is strongly recommended.

ollow the steps below for effective deep-frying:
) Heat 3–4 C oil in the wok until a light haze forms at approximately 375°F (190°C).
) Drop in foods and deep-fry until foods are cooked.
) Adjust the temperature to maintain a constant frying temperature of 375°F (190°C). Begin by set-ting temperature on high; if the oil gets too hot (smokes), turn down temperature to medium high and back to high if the oil drops below 375°F (190°C).
) Follow the instructions given in the recipe.

Roasting, Baking, or Broiling

hese cooking methods are so common and ordinary as to require limited explanation. Meats or rolls may be roasted or baked in the oven. When roasting meats, use a broiling pan or place rack on the bottom of a pan to support the meat. Add a small amount of water to the bottom of he pan, making sure the meat is above the water level. The water will keep the meat moist and also eep the drippings from burning onto the broiling pan.

ollow the steps below for effective roasting, baking or broiling:
) Preheat the oven to the required temperature.
) Place all foods in the center of the oven to allow for even roasting.
) Follow the instructions given in the recipe.

Steaming

teaming is one of the most nutritious, not to mention convenient, methods of cooking foods, retain-ng more nutrients and natural flavor than other conventional means of cooking. Steamed foods seal natural juices of meats and vegetables which are delicious served over rice.

here are many different types of steamers available. The wok with a cover will serve as a good steamer. Multi-tiered bamboo steamers may be purchased. However, a large pot with a cover will suffice for he purpose of steaming food.

teaming racks are required to support and elevate the plate or bowl which contains food to be steamed a wok. A round cake rack will serve just as well as commercially available steaming racks. You nay even improvise, using a water chestnut can with both ends removed as a substitute for a steam-ng rack. The rack should be set in the center of the wok or pan.

ll steamers operate according to the same basic principle. The efficient circulation of steam is of aramount importance. Bamboo steamers have several tiers in which many dishes can be steamed imultaneously. The tiers and cover are set on top of a wok containing boiling water. There are also netal steamers consisting of a pot to hold the water and usually two tiers and a cover. For example, he bottom pot functions to cook soup stock while the two tiers are used to steam two other separate ishes. In this manner, many dishes may be steamed at one time saving both time and energy.

ollow the steps below for effective steaming:
) Pour water in the wok or pot so that the water level stands one inch below the steaming rack or dish of food.
) Cover the wok and bring the water to a full boil.
) Use heatproof dishes only for steaming.
) Insert the dish of food atop the steaming rack. Cover and bring to full boil (or full steam) again. Turn the temperature down to medium high and allow to steam for the specified time.
) Check the water level when longer steaming times are necessary.

COOKING METHODS

Basic Cutting Methods

When preparing ingredients use a sharp knife. Cut to bite size pieces making them easy to cook and to eat.

For decorative cuts, use the tip of knife. For peeling use the lower part of blade. The part from the center towards the tip is used for most cutting techniques.

Rounds

Round ingredients such as *daikon* radish or carrot are cut into the same thickness.

Diagonal Slices

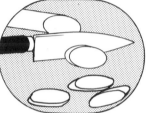

Thin round ingredients such as cucumber are sliced diagonally giving a large effect.

"Paring" Thin Fillets

Soft or fragile ingredients are placed flat and pared off with the knife parallel to the cutting board.

Quarter Rounds

Large round ingredients such as turnip or *daikon* radish are split into quarters and then sliced.

Half-rounds

Large round ingredients such as *daikon* radish are split into halves and sliced.

Wedges

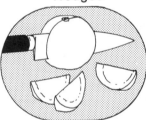

Ingredients such as lemon or onion are split into quarters then eighths.

Rolling Wedges

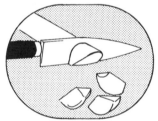

Ingredients are rolled and cut diagonally to give more sides for seasoning.

Rectangles

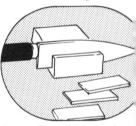

Large ingredients such a *daikon* radish are cut into 2 in (5cm) length and then sliced into ½ in (1.5cm) thickness.

Shreds

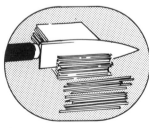

Ingredients are sliced into thin rectangles of 2-2½ in (5-6.5cm) length, layered and cut into thin match like sticks parallel to the fibers.

Sticks

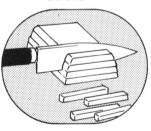

Ingredients such as potato, carrot or bamboo shoots are cut into 2-2½ in (5-6.5cm) long, ⅜ in (1cm) wide sticks.

Dices

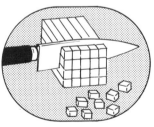

Ingredients are cut into ⅜ in (1cm) wide sticks, and then into ⅜ in (1cm) cubes.

Mincing

Shredded ingredients such as ginger root or green onion are chopped finely.

COOKING METHODS

How to Cook Rice

①MEDIUM HEAT UNTIL WATER BOILS

Cook rice over medium heat until water boils. Do not bring it to boiling point quickly. If the quantity of rice is large, cook rice over high heat from the beginning. The heat can be carried into the center of rice if cooked over medium heat.

②HIGH HEAT FOR 1 MINUTE AFTER BOILING

When it begins to a boil, turn heat to high and cook for 1 minute. Never lift lid while cooking.

③TURN HEAT TO LOW FOR 4–5 MINUTES

Turn heat to low and cook for 4–5 minutes (Be careful not to over-boil). Then the pot begins to steam.

④THE LOWEST HEAT FOR 10 MINUTES

Reduce heat to the lowest for 10 minutes. Every grain of rice absorbs water and becomes plump. It is liable to burn, so cook over the lowest heat.

⑤TURN OFF AND LET STAND FOR 10 MINUTES

Turn off the heat and let rice stand, covered for 10 minutes. During this 10 minutes the grains are allowed to "settle", and the cooking process is completed by the heat retained in the rice and the walls of the pot.

AUTOMATIC RICE COOKER

Today rice is cooked daily in many household in an automatic electric or gas rice cooker. The automatic rice cooker, an appliance developed in the postwar period, cooks perfect rice. Put washed rice in the cooker, add water. There are measurment marks in the cooker for water and rice volume. Then cover and turn on. Automatic controls take over cooking, reducing heat at exact time, and also in some models, the rice is kept warm till needed. Cookers come in various sizes, from tiny ones holding only a few cups to large ones used in restaurants. Automatic rice cookers, either electric or gas can be obtained at Asian stores.

UTENSILS

Wok

The Chinese wok is a round or flat-bottomed pan made of heavy gauge carbon steel. It comes in various sizes, but the most functional for our purposes is the 14 inch (35 cm) wok. The round-bottomed wok is usually accompanied by a ventilated ring which serves to support the base of the wok above a gas-range burner. A flat-bottomed wok, which does not require a ring stand, sits atop an electric range, but requires some adjustments during cooking as there is direct contact with the burner, resulting in much hotter temperatures.

When using a gas range, the ring should be situated with the sides slanting downwards and the smaller opening supporting the wok. The round-bottom design of the wok directs the heat source to the center of the wok which gets hot very quickly. The heat is then conducted rapidly and evenly throughout the rest of the wok. When using an electric range, the ring should be placed securely over the burner, with the sides slanting upwards to allow the center of the wok closer proximity to the burner.

Seasoning wok

Scrub the wok in hot sudsy water to remove the protective oil applied when manufactured. Rinse well and dry thoroughly. Season the cleaned wok by heating and rubbing a small amount of peanut oil on the inside surface with a paper towel. Re-heat the wok until hot and repeat the processs two more times. Your wok is now ready for use.

During the course of cooking a meal, the wok need only be cleaned with hot water, using a bristle scrub brush used for non-stick pans. When you are through using the wok, wash in sudsy water and rinse. Dry over medium heat and rub a dab of oil on the inside surface to prevent rust. Eventually, with constant use, your wok will assume a darker color on the inside which results in smooth non-stick cooking . Never scour your wok with harsh cleansers. If rust appears, simply scrub clean and reseason. Any time the wok is used for steaming, it must be reseasoned afterward in order afterwards prevent foods from sticking. However, only one coating of oil is necessary for reseasoning your wok.

Electric woks are good substitutes. They are especially suited for entertaining or cooking at the table. Just follow the package instructions for use and care.

Wok Accessories

Accessories specially designed for wok cooking are available in any cookware store. They greatly facilitate cooking with a wok.

Cover

The size of the dome-shaped cover depends largely upon the diameter of the wok. Sometimes a 10–12 inch (25–30 cm) cover to a frying pan may suffice. The convenience of a cover is readily apparent when it is necessary to steam ingredients using the wok.

Cleaver

The basic Chinese knife is the cleaver. It is used for cutting recipe ingredients and in the same motion transporting them to an awaiting wok or serving tray. The cleaver usually measures 3–4 inch (8–10 cm) wide and 8 inch (20 cm) long. The thickness varies from thin cleavers for vegetable slicing all the ay to thick bone-chopping cleavers. A sharp cleaver is necessary to perform the various cutting ethods discussed in the cooking methods section. Keep your cleaver sharp by using a sharpening one and steel as often as needed.

Curved Spatula

This utensil comes with a long handle with a wide, curved edge which fits the curved bottom of the wok. Ingredients can be more readily tossed and removed using a curved rather than straight-edged spatula.

Draining Rack

This wire semicircular rack attaches to the top of the wok. It is used in deep-frying to drain the oil from the food before removing onto a serving dish.

Wire Strainer, Fine Mesh Strainer

This strainer is made of wire with a long wooden handle. The large holes allow the ingredients to be removed quickly from hot oil, leaving the crumbs or bits of batter behind to be removed by a fine mesh strainer. It is also useful in removing large pieces of foods from soups or sauces.

Steaming Rack

This round rack, preferably made of metal, resembles a cake rack. It is used to elevate plates of food above the boiling water in a wok while steaming. Bamboo or metal steamers with two tiers and a cover are also available, but unless a lot of food is steamed, a wok and steaming rack is sufficient.

Deep-Frying Thermometer

This handy device will ensure the exact oil temperature used in recipes calling for deep-frying.

Cooking Chopsticks

These are longer than ordinary eating chopsticks. They are made of bamboo and come in various lengths. Choose the proper length by the omfort and ease of handling best suited to you. How to use:

. Rest the first chopstick on top of your ring finger with the thumb braced over the chopstick.

. Hold the other chopstick as you would a pencil.

. With the inside chopstick held stationary with your thumb, move the outside chopstick, forming pinchers to pick up ingredients.

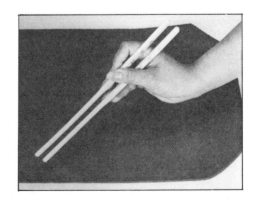

GLOSSARY

Anise, star
Brown, eight pointed star shaped seed with the taste of licorice. Used as a flavoring for sauce Keeps indefinitely on shelf.

Bamboo shoots
Cream colored, cone shaped shoots of bamboo. Canned shoots are most common. Once opene store covered with fresh water up to 1 week in the refrigerator. Change water frequentl Does not freeze well.

Bean curd, dried sheets or rolls
Sold in sheets or rolls. Soak in hot water until soft, rinse and cut into desired size befo using. Flat sheets can be deep fried, and soaked in hot water to soften before use. The shee become tougher, but will not dissolve with longer cooking, such as in braised dishes. Do n soak sheets in water before deep-frying.

Bean curd, fermented (fu yu)
Fermented white bean curd with a cheesy flavor. It is sold bottled in half inch thick square Keeps in refrigerator indefinitely after opening.

Bean curd, fresh (*tofu*)
Usually square shaped, creamy texture, bland curd made from soybeans. Also comes dee fried and canned. Fresh bean curd, covered with water, can be kept in the refrigerator fo approximately one week. Remove from original package and replace with fresh water as soo as possible. Change water every 2 days to keep fresh.

Bean curd, red (nam yu)
Sometimes called wet bean curd. Red soft cubes of fermented bean curd with a strong chees flavor. Comes in cans. Once opened, store in jars with a tight lid in the refrigerator indefinitel

Bean filling, sweet
Thick sweet bean paste made from beans and sugar. Often used as a filling for pastries. Usuall sold in cans. Store tightly covered in refrigerator or in freezer indefinitely.

Bean sauce, brown or yellow
Sauce made from soybeans and salt. Often comes in cans. Some bean sauces may contai bean halves and others may be a smooth sauce, similar to Japanese red *miso*, which can b used as a substitute in some recipes. Keeps indefinitely in the refrigerator in a tightly sealed ja

Bean threads (saifun or cellophane noodles)
Thin, long, dry noodles made of mung bean flour. Keeps on shelf indefinitely. Soak in warr water for 15 minutes before use. May also be deep-fried in hot oil. Do not soak in water used for deep-frying. Use as a noodle in soups or with stir fried vegetables and meats. T keep clean up to a minimum, place noodles in a large paper bag before removing wrappe Break off amount needed and store remainder in bag.

Bean paste, hot (soy bean paste with crushed red chili)
Soybean sauce made from soybeans, chili peppers and sometimes garlic. Comes in cans c jars. Refrigerated, keeps indefinitely in tightly sealed jars. Degree of hotness may vary betwee different brands. Brown soybean sauce combined with a hot sauce or crushed red chill ca be used as a substitute.

ean sprouts
prouts of the mung bean: about 2 inch (5 cm) long. Refrigerate sprouts covered with water.
eeps for one week. Change the water often.

itter melon
ong, green, pear shaped melon with a ridged surface. It has a definite bitter taste. Cut mel-
n in half lengthwise and remove seeds. Cut in thin slices and stir-fry with meats.

lack beans, fermented
alted, fermented, soft black bean seed. Mainly used to flavor sauces. Rinse with water be-
re using. Keeps in a covered container on the shelf indefinitely.

lack bean sauce with chili
alted, fermented black beans combined with hot chili peppers often found in paste form.

ok choy (Chinese cabbage or greens)
ark green leafy vegetable with a white stalk. Keeps in refrigerator for one week. High in
itamins A and C.

roccoli, Chinese
tender, green, seasonal vegetable available in spring and summer months. Chinese broc-
oli is more slender and leafy than regular broccoli. For recipes in this book, substitute with
ok choy, spinach, or regular broccoli cut into long slender pieces.

leaver
he knife used to do most cutting in Chinese cooking. Usually a lighter, thinner cleaver is
sed for slicing and chopping meats and vegetables. The heavier cleaver is used to cut through
one.

loud ears
rown, irregular, leafy shaped fungus or mushroom with a delicate taste. Soak 15 minutes
warm water to soften. Rinse, remove hard knobs on bottom of ear before using. Keeps
definitely on shelf when dried. Also called tree ears.

ive spice
lend of five ground spices: Szechuan peppercorns, anise, cinnamon, fennel and cloves. Keeps
n shelf for several months.

inger root
regular bulb, (rhizome) of the ginger plant. Hot and spicy in taste. Slice ginger and freeze
eparated slices. Keeps in the freezer indefinitely. Peel ginger and store in rice wine, or sim-
ly wrap air tight cintainer and store in refrigerator.
lice and use as needed.

airy melon (jit gwa)
val shaped, green melon with a hairy surface. Peel, slice thin and use in soup.

oisin sauce
ungent, sweet condiment sauce made of soybeans, spices, chili and sugar. Once opened,
tore in a jar with tight lid. Keeps refrigerated for about 6 months.

elly fish
ody of the jelly fish cut into shreds. Usually sold salted and packaged in plastic bags in
he refrigerator section. Store in refrigerator or freezer. Rinse off salt and soak in cold water
efore using.

GLOSSARY

Litchi nuts
A sweet, white fruit about 1 inch (2.5 cm) in diameter. It has a dark red hull which mus be removed before eating. Also comes canned and dried. Use as garnish or as a fruit.

Long beans, Chinese
Foot long, thin green beans. When cooked, resemble string beans but have a more delicat flavor. Treat in same manner as regular green beans, but requires much less cooking time

Maifun (rice noodles)
Noodles made from rice flour. Soak until soft in hot water before using. Also, noodles ma be deep-fried in hot oil. Do not soak before deep-frying. To keep clean up to a minimum place package of noodles in a large paper bag before removing wrapper. Break off amount as needed. Store remainder in the bag.

Mirin
Japanese sweet rice wine used in cooking to bring out flavor or to add a little sweetness Not interchangeable with rice wine.

Miso
Fermented bean paste made from soybeans and rice. Used mainly in Japanese cooking. Rec or *aka miso* is saltier and white or *shiro miso* is milder or sweeter. Red *miso* is a good substitute for brown bean sauce. Refrigerate *miso* in sealed containers indefinitely.

Mushroom, dried (forest or black)
Dried black forest mushrooms have a delicate flavor. Can be stored in covered container o the shelf, indefinitely. Must soak in warm water until soft, rinse, discard stem and use in recipe

Mustard, dried
Pungent powder. When mixed with water, forms sauce which is used as a dip to accompany barbecued pork and other foods. Store dry powder on shelf indefinitely. Mix 1 T water to 1 T dry powder for average proportion.

Orange peel
Dried peel of tangerines. Used for flavoring meats and other dishes. To prepare: Thoroughly clean skin of tangerine, peel into sections, cut away pulp and allow skin to sun dry. Make sure skin is free of pesticides if making your own dried skins.

Oyster sauce
Thick brown sauce made from oysters and soy sauce. Used to enhance flavor or as a dip Keeps indefinitely in the refrigerator.

Panko (dehydrated bread crumbs)
Japanese dehydrated bread crumbs with a coarser texture than regular bread crumbs. Avail able at most supermarkets or oriental groceries. To make *panko*, use white bread and make coarse crumbs in the blender. Then dry crumbs slightly in the oven. Then, dry crumbs slightly in oven.

Parsley, Chinese (Coriander or cilantro)
A leafy parsley with a pungent flavor. Use as a garnish. Also may be used to add flavor to most any dish.

Plum sauce
A sauce made from plums and apricots combined with vinegar, sugar and chili pepper. Use as a dip for roast duck or meat dishes.

GLOSSARY

ice

ong grain is most popular among southern Chinese. Calrose, medium grain rich can be used
s substitute. Glutinous rice is very sticky when cooked and is used for sweets. Refer to rice
ection for more information.

ausage, Chinese (Lop cheong)

ured pork sausages about 6 inches (15 cm) in length with a sweet flavor. Refrigerate up to
ne month or freeze up to several months.

eaweed, dried

ried seaweed is usually available in sheets. Keeps indefinitely on the shelf. Some seaweed
neets are more expensive because they are roasted and seasoned. These are used in Japanese
uisine for *sushi*.

esame seed oil

olden brown oil of toasted sesame seeds. Buy in small quantities and keep refrigerated af-
·r opening. Add to dishes just before serving, loses flavor when heated.

hrimp, dried

ried tiny shrimp. Soak in warm water for about $1/2$ hour to soften before use. Keep on shelf
ndefintely in covered jars.

now ear

/hite fungus or mushroom. Comes dried and must be soaked in warm water before use.
emove hard knobs from bottom of ears. Keeps dried indefinitely.

now peas (Chinese pea pods)

lat edible pea pod. Has a delicate taste and comes fresh or frozen. Must string as in green
eans before cooking.

oy sauce

he extract of fermented soybeans combined with salt. Soy sauce range from light to dark
ight soy sauce is the most delicate, and is used as dip or in cooking; gives little color. Some
ark soy sauce has caramel added for color and is slightly sweet. Japanese soy sauce is in
ne middle and serves most purposes very well. For most recipes, Japanese soy sauce may
e used unless specified differently in a recipe.

zechuan peppercorns (fagara)

ried berry of the prickly ash. It is not hot but has a slow numbing effect. Lightly toast
a fry pan; finely crush to a powder. Strain through a fine mesh strainer to filter coarse outer
nell.

zechuan vegetable

he knobby bulb of a radish preserved in chili pepper and salt. Rinse before using. Store
irtight in jar. Refrigerate or freeze indefinitely. No substitutes.

apioca starch

·r flour is used in the making of certain types of dim sum. It is also sometimes used as
 thickening agent. It is sold in most Asian grocery stores. It will keep for several months
a a dry place.

iger lily flowers

·ried golden brown tiger lily flowers; about 2 inches (5 cm) long. Soak in warm water about
5 minutes and rinse, remove hard stem before use. Keeps indefinitely on shelf when dry.

GLOSSARY

Thickening, cornstarch and water

Cornstarch and water is the most popular mixture used to thicken a sauce. Dissolve tablespoon of cornstarch in 1 tablespoons of water. Use as needed to thicken sauce to th desired consistency. Always bring sauce to a full boil and then thoroughly combine ingr dients together.

Freshest ingredients of the season, attention to the technique of stir-frying, cooking just u til crisp and tender and most importantly be consistent and organized.

Tonkatsu sauce

Japanese prepared sauce used as a dip for _tonkatsu_, a pork cutlet.

Turnip, Chinese (lo bok or _daikon_)

Crisp large whith root vegetable resembling a large carrot. Peel skin and slice or shred b fore using. Store in refrigerator.

Turnip, salted-turnip

Sliced and preserved with salt. Rinse off salt before using. Often used in fillings or slice and steamed with pork. Keeps in tightly sealed jar indefinitely.

Vinegar, rice

A mild vinegar made from rice. Used in most oriental dishes. Keeps indefinetly on shel

Water chestnuts

Walnut size, brown bulb. Must be peeled before use. It is sweet and has a crisp texture sim lar to apples. Canned water chestnuts are peeled and boiled. They will keep, if covered wit fresh water in the refrigerator for about 2 weeks. Change the water frequently.

Wheat starch

A special flour used in the making of certain types of dumplings. This type of flour is avail ble in Asian groceries. It is not interchangeable with other types of flour as it produces specific texture. Wheat starch keeps for several months kept in a dry place.

Wine lees

A thick fermented wine paste. Light _miso_ (Japanese soybean paste) can be used as a subst tute. _Sake_ is a good substitute.

Wine, Shaohsing or rice

Chinese rice wine used for drinking or cooking. Dry sherry may be used as a substitut

Winter melon (tung gwa)

A large light green melon with a white powdery surface resembling a water melon. The i side is white with seeds in the center. Usually sold in sections. Peel hard skin and discar seeds. Slice melon and use in soups.

Wok

A wok is a metal pan with sloping sides and a rounded or flat bottom. The 14 inche (35 cm wok is the best size for home use. Refer to wok in the information section of this book (pag 96). My personal preference is the 14 inches (35 cm) flat bottom wok.

Won tons

Fresh squares of noodle. Usually comes in one pound packages. Thickness varies from thic to thin. Fresh won tons will keep in the refrigerator for one week. Can be frozen, wrappe airtight, for about 2 months. Use thick wrappers for deep fried won tons. Thin wrapper are better for soups.

INDEX